Professional Stockmaking

Through the Eyes of a Stockmaker

by

David L. Wesbrook

Professional Stockmaking

©2015 by David L. Wesbrook.
All rights reserved.

All rights reserved under International and Pan-American Copyright Conventions. No part of this book may be reproduced in any form or by an electronic or mechanical means, including information storage and retrieval systems, without permission in writing from the publisher.

Printed in the United States of America
20 19 18 17 16   5 4 3 2 1

Published 1994
Reprinted July 2015

ISBN: 1-879356-15-5

ISBN: 978-1-879356-15-3

Wolfe Publishing Company
2180 Gulfstream, Suite A
Prescott, Arizona 86301

FOREWORD

Gunmaking books, while they treat a very specialized subject, long have made up at least a portion of the offering of publishers whose purview tends to encompass how-to-do-it subjects. Some of these books have been useful, while others have left a myriad of questions unanswered, or worse, presented questionable techniques. The truth of the matter is that it is difficult to locate a stockmaker or artisan of any sort that can find the time to compose a serious book and has the ability to do so. Long days of meticulous and exacting benchwork do not turn the prospect of bookwriting into thrilling evening entertainment. This, of course, is vastly compounded by the need for illustration, and that means photography which must be shot while work is underway at the bench, miles and miles of film. In order to complete a book that has adequate illustration, it's necessary for the gunmaker to do the photography himself rather than relying upon a photographer from outside to drop by just when a certain procedure needs to be shot. And that aspect of making a book can slow bench production to a point that the stockmaker's kids may find themselves weakly grousing over who gets to divide the last pole bean, while the mailbox fills with flaming letters from irate patrons who want their new rifle in time for elk season. It's a wonder then, that we have *any* gunmaking books containing anything other than the most cursory glances at the trade. Romantic and sweeping overviews may provide entertaining reading for the armchair gunstocker, but not for the serious gunmaker who needs facts, and a great number of them at that.

Far and away the greatest number of gunmaking titles produced by any publisher to date were the excellent books from Tom Samworth's Small-Arms Technical Publishing Company in South Carolina. From well before World War II until the 1950s, essential and even pioneering books such as Clyde Baker's *Modern Gunsmithing*, R.H. Angier's *Firearm Blueing and Browning*, W.F. Vickery's *Advanced Gunsmithing*, Newell's *Gunstock Finishing and Care*, Monty Kennedy's *Gunstock Checkering and Carving*, and Roy Dunlap's *Gunsmithing* flowed from Samworth's small but keenly tuned operation. Along with these were other classic works which included C.S. Landis' *Twenty-Two Caliber Varmint Rifles* and other seminal titles on the design and use of sporting arms by Townsend Whelen, Julian Hatcher, E.C. Crossman, and Elmer Keith. Samworth didn't ignore earlier works of merit, either, such as A.C. Gould's 1892 *Modern American Rifles*, which he reprinted in 1946. We owe Samworth a great debt for his large and rich array of gun books, especially since there are relatively few publishers today willing to undertake such highly specialized and expensive-to-produce titles that have relatively limited markets.

Something else that we owe to Tom Samworth was his ability to coax gunmakers into writing extensive treatises on their art. One author that Samworth himself must have considered the greatest character among a cast of undisputed nonconformists was Alvin Linden, a fine gunmaker in Wisconsin who was one of the pioneers in the development of the American classic gunstock. With Samworth's urging, Linden began compiling his three-volume *Firearm Design & Assembly* by 1941, completing it after the War. The work contains complete essays on inletting, shaping and finishing liberally sprinkled with wry humor and sharp criticism of mediocrity wherever the author found it. Something of the Mark Twain of the gunmaking world, Linden loved to puncture sacred cows. In fact, he did not spare himself his usual dose of tongue-in-cheek verbal abuse, constantly referring to his own work as that of a "woodbutcher." Nevertheless, his insistence upon sound and workmanlike quality is clearly evident through his constant patter of folksy homily. Linden made a great show of caring not for what others thought of his brand of instruction. "No doubt you have heard about the folly of tossing pearls before four-footed porkers," he observed. "Well, they would at least grunt their appreciation — and the pearls could be salvaged, none the worse for wear and tear." The "porkers," if we are to believe the Old Swede, had more perception than the woodbutchers of the 1940s. We have a different sort of herd awaiting such pearls today, people willing to do more than grunt in appreciation.

Al Linden's books were the most thorough essays on centerfire stockmaking written until now, yet they were never reprinted. The books were largely illustrated with line drawings by Linden, supplemented by a few good halftones. Despite the excellent full-scale foldouts provided, the work — like most other gunsmithing treatises of the time — suffered from the relatively small number of illustrations needed to supplement the wordy text. Nevertheless, Linden managed to get across the word, and in doing so largely followed an ancient tradition in gunmaking. He emphasized, for example, the use of edge tools such as planes and drawknives in stock shaping, and hammered the reader with the necessity of developing stock architecture in a series of converging lines, bevels, and flats. In short, he knew that a successful gunstock was the result of understanding a system of linear and curvilinear geometry. He saw the gunstock as a piece of functional sculpture, and he had an almost unconscious understanding of the relationship of eye and traditional tools to the finished product.

Dave Wesbrook has carried Linden's insightful study to a considerably greater height with this book, and in doing so has provided the stockmaker with instruction never brought together in such a comprehensive fashion. Aside from Dave's personal views of careful perfection — indeed the hallmark of any fine gunstocker — he has compiled what rightly should be considered a stockmaking textbook by virtue of the numerous exceptional halftones which accompany the text. A picture may be worth a thousand words, but it must contain exquisite detail to do so, and the author — well known as a consummate master of arms photography — has not stinted in this. And in regard to words, the text outlines sound methodology and a logical selection of tools well enough that even seasoned professionals will discover useful tricks they had not known before. The fledgling stockmaker is presented with a program of stockmaking and finishing far more complete than even the best gunmaking seminars or workshops could possibly provide.

Despite the necessarily forthright presentation of workmanship presented here, I still detect that certain sense of humility almost always present in the demeanor of any skilled artisan who, while confident in his ability, is never quite satisfied with his own efforts. Such individuals usually are filled with curiosity and excitement about fine work, both old and new, or they tend to be ever open to learning a better way. That is a good thing, for people such as this — the Dave Wesbrooks and others like him — inevitably discover the great pleasure of sharing the "art and mystery" of the trade. Such instruction, of course, is no matter of small responsibility. Although Dave discusses techniques with which he has become comfortable over the years, he is quick to observe that other stockmakers utilize different methods equally as valid. And he generously illustrates this with essays by other gunmakers, each well-known in their own right.

Most importantly, there is the logic and natural progression to Dave's instruction that is absolutely necessary to the production of a fine centerfire stock, whether shaped "from the stick" or finished from a precision-machined blank. With perhaps the exception of a cheek-stock wheellock or the buttstock of a curvaciously Schoyen-like offhand schuetzen, nowhere could one encounter a more complex gunstock design to fabricate than that of the modern classic sporter. Even the finest stock machining imaginable will not prevent a gunstocker's work from regressing from silk purse to sow's ear unless a critical perception of utility and the proportion and flow of graceful architecture are present. Here, these things are made evident in a fashion never before so illuminating, and couched withal in an essential understanding of traditional methods that we have tended to "lose," such as the logical use of bench planes. Al Linden no doubt would have observed that when we try to re-invent the wheel with newfangled techniques, it tends to come out octagonal, or worse. Dave inserts no such sharp Lindenesque derision for skewed working attitudes, nor has he any need of doing so. Nevertheless, despite the lack of textual barbs, I have no doubt whatsoever that Al would have been quite proud to put his own name on this book.

—*John Bivins*
Wilmington, N.C.

The author photographing a stock.

INTRODUCTION

Author's note: Dr. Edward C. Ezell, curator of the National Firearms Collection at the Smithsonian Institution, authority on small arms, and friend, had originally offered to write the introduction to this book. Ed died on December 23, 1993 after a two year battle with cancer of the kidney.

Although he was thoroughly familiar with the contents of the book, he asked me to put some of my personal thoughts on paper as an aid to his writing the introduction. The following letter was written two months prior to his death.

I believe that Ed would have used much of what was contained in this letter in his introduction. It is therefore appropriate that this letter be reprinted here.

I shall miss you my friend — David.

Ed,

Like you, when John Bivins published his series of articles on gunmaking I looked at John as sort of a hero. Not only did he freely give of his knowledge, but by example he also challenged all gunmakers to elevate their craft to new levels of excellence.

For a craft to grow knowledge must be shared among any and all who wish to learn. Without this sharing a craft will eventually stagnate and die. Technological advances in the production of one-to-one wood duplicating machines have kept the craft of stockmaking alive during recent years, but at a cost. That cost was in terms of both the styling and, perhaps more importantly, the understanding of the stock ergonomics necessary for the most efficient use of the gun in the field. In fact, a large percentage of the custom rifles produced in this country in the last ten years or so have been nothing more than stylized clones of rifles made by Jerry Fisher, Al Biesen, or Dale Goens. These rifles all had standard dimensions for the length of pull and drop at the heel and comb. The "one size fits all" approach to gunmaking. As a result, today few gunmakers in understand how the fit of the stock affects its function. Take for example the "pitch" of a stock. Few stockmakers can even define pitch let alone tell you its function. (Quite simply, pitch is the angle across the end of the butt, relative to the boreline, necessary to firmly fit the butt of the rifle to the shooter's shoulder when the rifle is held with the boreline parallel to the ground.) In fact, the three major books on gunsmithing written this century (Clyde Baker, James Howe, and Roy Dunlop) offered neither a satisfactory explanation of pitch *or* its function. Many other areas of stockmaking were also either skimmed over or neglected entirely. I am sure that each of these men knew what pitch was, but simply didn't stop to analyze its function in relation to fitting the stock to the physical characteristics of the individual shooter or to the relationship that the pitch plays in the transfer of the recoil from the rifle to the shooter's shoulder.

This is important stuff, Ed. If the rifle is not properly fit to the shooter, the overall function of the rifle is greatly impaired. The English shotgun stockmakers understand this. Unfortunately, few of either the English or Americans that stock bolt action rifles do. At least none of those who do understand it have ever written about it.

I believe, I hope, that this book has avoided many of the shortcomings and pitfalls of the previous books on stockmaking. By writing the book as a step-by-step photo essay with commentary I have tried to isolate and analyze each stage of the stockmaking process. Designing a camera boom that positioned the camera at any point over the bench allowed me to photograph each step of the process from the same perspective that the individual doing the work would see. I hope the combination of the two makes up for any deficiency in one or the other.

The work was conceived and written as a two-volume set. The first volume contains books 1-3 which cover the inletting of the semi-inletted stock, the finish shaping, and the sanding and stock finishing. The second volume contains books 4-7 which cover the design and layout of the square blank stock, inletting the square blank, rough shaping, and checkering. The two volumes contain approximately 700 pages and 500 photographs. That there exists a great need for a book such as this is demonstrated by the willingness of men such as yourself, John, Monte, and a half dozen other gunmakers to take time away from the bench in order to make suggestions and contribute specific sections to the text.

I suspect that the original motivation for writing the book was one of self-promotion. As the work progressed into months and then years that attitude changed. I realized that no analytic or comprehensive book on the subject had ever been written, and that anyone wanting to learn the craft had to do so, for the most part, through trial and error. At this point my motives for finishing the book turned more toward altruism and stewardship.

Now, after having worked on it off and on for almost 11 years, I just want to get the damn thing done. I suppose that I will feel a sense of accomplishment when the last word is written and the last page of layout is done. More realistically, as you well know, Ed, there will be a sense of relief.

This letter is long, rambling, and not very well written, but I hope it helps you in writing the introduction.

David

CONTENTS

Foreword iii

Introduction ix

Book I
Introduction to Inletting the Semi-inletted Stock

Introduction to Inletting 7
    Definition of inletting - Inletting black - Patience - Workbench -
    Tools - Types of lighting

Inletting the Trigger Guard/Magazine Box into a Semi-inletted Stock 10
    Alignment and initial fit - Inletting the corners of the box -
    Flat scraper - Trigger-guard tangs - Outside radius at rear of box -
    Proper clearance between box and action

Inletting the Barreled Action — Section 1

Rough Inletting 26
    Inletting guide screws - Leveling - Outlining barreled action onto
    stock - Choosing the right chisel - Rough inletting the half-inch
    barrel channel - Repair of mistakes - Alternate methods for
    difficult wood - Barrel channel rasp

Rough Inletting the Barrel Channel with the in-cannel Gouges 40
    Muscle control - Hand positions - Control of fine cuts

Inletting the Barreled Action Semi-inlet — Section 2

Finish Inletting 48
    Insertion and removal of barreled action from the stock -

Marking points of contact - Chisels - Flat scrapers - Tang -
Curved sidewalls of receiver - Recoil lug mortise - Receive ring -
Fisher Inletting scrapers - Barrel channel scrapers - Half depth
determination - Inletting complete

Book II
Finish Shaping the Stock

Introduction to Finish Shaping 77
    Definitions - Line flow diagrams - Stages of shaping -
    Design history - Lighting

Section 1 - Fitting the stock to the individual shooter 84
    Physical characteristics of the shooter versus stock fit - Stock
    dimensions - Length of pull - Location of grip - Drop at heel
    and comb - Cast-off - Pitch - Toe-out

Section 2 - Introduction to the tools used in shaping 98
    The smooth-cut plane - Palm plane - Bull nose plane -
    The spokeshave - The In-cannel gouge - The straight chisels -
    Nicholson 50 rasp - Crossing file

Section 3 - Shaping begins - profiling the buttstock 130
    Toeline - Nose of Comb - Top of wrist - Modification of Tang -
    Sides of grip

Section 4 - Shaping the sides of the buttstock 138
    Line flow diagram - Right side of buttstock - Toe-line - Top and
    sides of comb-line - Left side of buttstock - Shaping areas adjacent
    to the cheekpiece - Ghostline of cheekpiece - Cheekpiece fluting

Section 5 - Rough shaping the combnose
fluting, the top and upper sides of the wrist 170
    Comb nose fluting and tip of wrist - Pistol grip and finger
    clearance arch

Section 6 - Shaping the body and forearm of the stock 184
    Body - Profiling the forearm - Rough shaping the forearm - Finish shaping the forearm - Ejection port and bolt handle recess

Book III
Sanding and Stock Finishing

Sanding - Section 1 197
    Right Side of the Buttstock - Side Profile Line of the Wrist - Lower Right Side of the Butt and Lower Rear Portion of the Grip - Toe-line and the Small Radius at the Rear of the Grip - Lower Left Side of the Buttstock and Grip - Behind and Below the Cheekpiece - Front of the Cheekpiece - The Cheekpiece - Front of the Grip - finger Clearance Arch - Upper Wrist and the Comb Nose Fluting - Body the the Stock Through the Receiver Area - Forearm

Stock Finishing - Section 2 246
    Stock finishing essays by Dave Wesbrook, Monte Mandarino, Mark Silver, Ed Webber, Richard Schreiber, and Bruce Farnam

Appendix I

Inletting a Steel Buttplate 281
    Curved Sides of the Plate - Cutting in the Tit of the Buttplate - Spotting-In - Use of a Curved Riffler - Use of the Flat Scraper - Inletting Completed - Layout of a Skeleton Buttplate - Grinding the Draft

Appendix II

Tools Used in Stockmaking 303
    Channels - Gouges - In-cannel Gouges

Acknowledgements 308

DEDICATION

This book is dedicated
to the memory of my parents
Mr. Elmer E. and Mrs. Ruth L. Wesbrook.

Thank you for supporting the child
who walked a different path,
and for teaching me that anything
worth doing was worth doing well.

PROFESSIONAL STOCKMAKING

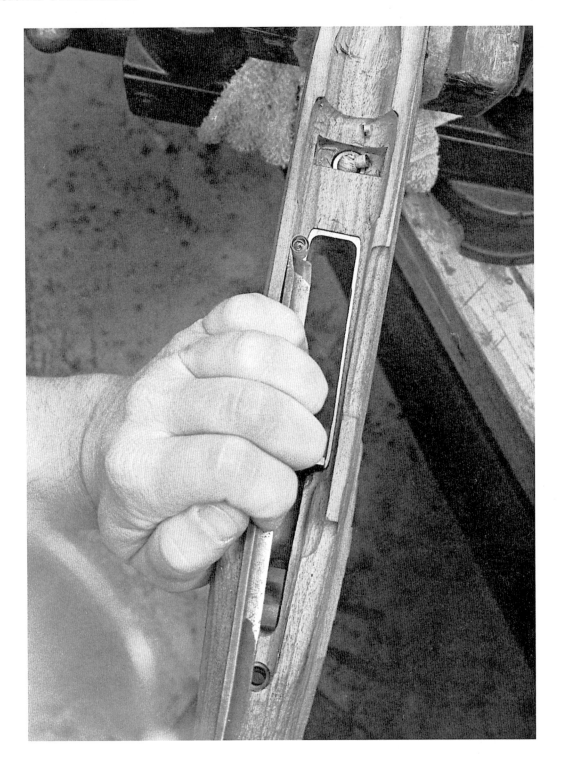

Figure 1-1 is the reason for the book's subtitle Through the Eyes of a Stockmaker. *The fuzzy area in the lower left encompasses the author's right eyebrow and glasses. Note the long curl of wood at the end of the 5/8-inch incannel gouge. Cuts like these are only possible with razor-sharp tools and proper tool technique.*

BOOK I

INTRODUCTION TO INLETTING THE SEMI-INLETTED STOCK

The inletting of a gunstock is the precise fitting of the metal and wooden components of the rifle into one functional unit. It is accomplished through the careful use of chisels, scrapers, and inletting black. The function of the inletting is to secure the metal to the wood in such a way that the metal is supported evenly, yet firmly, at specific contact points.

In general, the areas of the inletting that must be in full contact with the metal are the bottom of the receiver and the rear surface of the recoil lug; all other rear-facing surfaces should be relieved slightly. (The exceptions are the kidney-shaped areas at the rear of the Mauser receiver which help absorb and transmit the shock of recoil to the stock, and the ends of the Mauser and Springfield magazine boxes, which should be fit tightly to help support the recoil abutments of the action.) The top edge of the inletting should be fit tightly enough to prevent debris and water from entering, but not so tightly that uneven pressure is induced against the sides of the barrel or receiver. The tools and procedures for inletting each area of the stock will be discussed in their respective turn.

A spotting agent, Jerrow's Inletting Black, is used during the inletting process to show the points of contact between the metal and wood. At each point of contact a small amount of wood is removed and the metal work is again inserted into the stock to mark new points of contact.

It would be nice if one could follow the steps in the section on inletting in precise numerical sequence and thereby complete the entire job of inletting. However, due to variations of dimension within the same style actions, differences in barrel contours, tolerances of the pre-inletted mortices and other factors, the finish inletting of a pre-inletted (semi-finished) stock is not as simple as following a set number or sequence of steps. Rather, the process must be treated as a whole, with random attention paid to each point of contact indicated by the transfer of inletting black.

The first trial fitting of the metal and wood may show two or three areas of contact that need a small amount of wood removed. An increasing number of contact points will be seen as the inletting proceeds and the metal is lowered deeper into the wood. Once again, a small amount of wood needs to be removed at each point and the process repeated until the metal reaches its final depth and the inletting process is complete. Depending on the tolerances of the pre-inletted mortice, the entire inletting process can take as few as a couple of dozen trial fittings to perhaps several times that number.

Patience, the supreme virtue of the stockmaker, allows him to repeatedly remove only the thinnest of shavings from each area until eventually the entire barreled action settles into its final position. Inletting is not the type of work that can be done quickly. The finished product will reflect the amount of time and care put into it.

Good inletting requires total concentration on the task at hand. Any slip of the tools can result in an unsightly gap between the metal and the wood, which at best looks bad and at worst will structurally weaken a critical area of the stock. While doing the inletting you should lock the door to the shop, send the wife out shopping and the kids out to play, and the dog to his corner of the shop. Concentrating on any subject is hard enough, but the total concentration that is needed to produce good inletting comes only after the first hour or so of continuous work. Any interruption, will break that total concentration and it will take another hour of work before you get it back again.

A sturdy workbench and a heavy vise with padded jaws are required for stock work. In fact, the bigger and heavier these two accessories are, the better, as we need to support the stock as steadily as possible while it is being worked on. The vise in the illustrations is a specialized woodworking vise that has both articulated jaws for holding oddly shaped objects and a swiveling base that allows the work to be swung out from the bench for easier access to all areas of the stock.

A word about tools is in order

here. Buy the best that you can afford. A good chisel will hold its edge throughout an entire inletting job. Controlled cutting with a chisel requires that the cutting edge is razor sharp. Nothing is more conducive to poor inletting than a dull chisel that tears and compresses the wood instead of cutting cleanly through it. Pamphlets on sharpening small tools are available from gunsmithing supply houses and companies specializing in woodworking tools. These pamphlets offer valuable hints and techniques on sharpening.

Now a word about lighting. The ability to properly light the work is necessary to produce good inletting. Quite simply, you have to be able to see the contours of a shape in order to shape it.

The best lighting that I have found for inletting, shaping, and sanding is one of the swing-arm lamps available from hardware and office supply stores. To be most efficient in use, the lamp should be mounted on the wall behind the bench and approximately 18 inches higher than the benchtop.

This lamp swings on an arm and the light can be directed to wherever it is needed. Swinging the lamp side to side or up and down allows the stockmaker to light every corner of the inletting and create the shadows needed to give the work the three-dimensional quality necessary to show the contours of the area being worked on. A 60- or 75-watt bulb provides all the light needed and is less fatiguing to the eyes than the brighter bulbs. Because this lamp is positioned in close to the work, and also to the worker's eyes, it is wise to extend the shade of the lamp a few inches by taping a piece of cardboard or construction paper to the outside of the lamp. (NOTE: Each individual perceives the quality and quantity of light differently, therefore experimentation with different types of lighting is a must. Work with the light source and brightness that works best for you.)

Inletting the Trigger Guard/Magazine Box into a Semi-Inletted Stock

Figures 1-2 through 1-13

When inletting a Mauser or Springfield action, in which the magazine box and trigger guard are of one-piece construction, this assembly is inletted first. If you are stocking a Winchester Model 70, a Sako, or a Remington 700, which have a three-piece trigger guard, the barreled action is inletted first, but you should still review the information contained in this section prior to beginning the inletting of the barreled action.

Begin by coating the trigger guard assembly (called "the guard," for short) with a thin layer of inletting black. The thinner the coating, the better. After the initial coat has been brushed on, it is seldom necessary or advisable to add more black to the coated surface. By continually brushing out the original coat after each trial fitting, a thinner, more uniform coat is achieved, which results in a more accurate transfer of the black to the wood, and more accurate inletting.

Then, making sure that the front and rear tangs of the guard are positioned correctly above their respective mortices in the stock, carefully align the magazine box with its precut mortice and lower it into the wood until it stops. At those places where the box contacts the wood, small spots of black will transfer to the surface of the inletting. The guard is then lifted out of the stock and a small amount of wood is removed at each point of contact. The process is repeated until the metal has been inletted even with, or slightly below the surface of the wood.

NOTE: On most actions the front and rear of the magazine box form a 90-degree angle with the bottom of the receiver, and the bottom of the guard slopes slightly downward from the rear tang toward the front of the rifle. In order to maintain the proper position of the guard in relation to the precut action inletting, and to ensure the proper feeding of cartridges from the magazine, these angles must be maintained as the inletting progresses. Also, care must be taken that the metal is both fit and removed from the stock with as little side-to-side or front-to-back rocking movement as possible. Rocking the guard results in a false transfer of the inletting black to the wood which, when wood is removed at each of these points, may leave gaps between the metal and the wood. The inletting at the front and sides of the box and at the ends of the tangs is especially susceptible to gaps resulting from the false transfer of the inletting black.

In Figure 1-2, the magazine box has been lowered into its mortice to check the initial alignment and fit. In most instances the box will drop part way into the pre-inletted mortice without any need to remove wood. If not, usually the wood at the corners of the magazine box mortice must be removed in order for the box to start to enter into its precut mortice. There are two ways to approximate the amount of wood to remove at this stage. The first is to make

Figure 1-2

a paper template of the top of the magazine box (the part closest to the action). Align the front of the template with the front of the mortice and use a sharp pencil to trace the radii of the corners of the box onto the wood. The second method is to use the box itself as a template and simply trace around it. In either instance, these outlines only provide an approximation of the position of the finished inletting and you should remove only enough wood to allow the box to start into the pre-cut mortice.

A 1/4-inch in-cannel gouge and a No. 9, 5mm Swiss carving gouge are used to remove the wood from the front and rear radii of the magazine box mortice. When cutting such a radius it is best to use a chisel that has slightly more curvature than that of the radius being cut. (Chisel selection and tool technique are discussed in Figures 1-17 and 1-18.)

Inletting the Semi-inletted Stock

The author's hunting rifle for several years. 7x57 Mauser; weight 6-3/4 lbs. loaded, magazine capacity 3 rounds. Shotgun-style trigger guard with tang extended down the front of the grip to the grip cap. Single set/single pull trigger by Mr. Jack Haugh. Griffin & Howe-style cheek piece

Figure 1-3

Figure 1-3 illustrates the contact points between the metal and wood as they appear during one of the initial fittings. The wood at the front radius of the magazine box is removed with a 1/4-inch cannel gouge. The chisel is held vertically in one hand and the fingers of the other hand position and guide the chisel in a series of small cuts around the inside of the radius. (Also see Figure 1-11 for hand positioning and instructions on cutting inside radii with an in-cannel gouge.)

The mark toward the rear of the magazine mortice, left by the small radius between the side and the back of the box, is cut away using a No. 9, 5mm Swiss Carving gouge (See "arrow" in Figure 1-3). The inletting black on the sides of the magazine box mortice is removed with scrapers as shown in Figure 1-4.

Inletting the Semi-inletted Stock

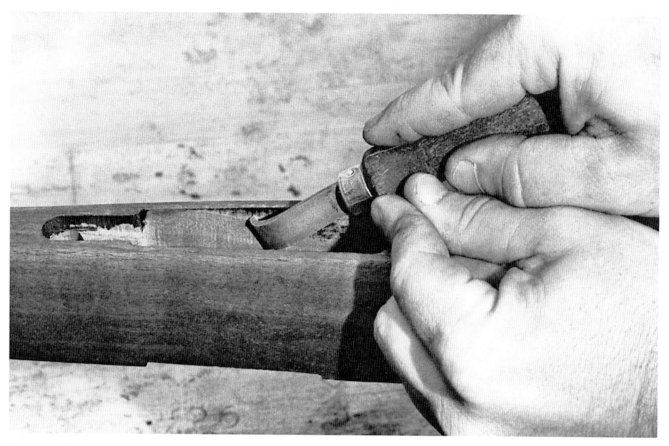

Figure 1-4

In Figure 1-4, a flat scraper is used to remove the inletting black (and a small amount of wood) from the side of the magazine box mortice. Scrapers are useful tools that remove a very controlled amount of wood while leaving a smooth surface to the wood. In use, the tool is held in one hand with the fingers of the other hand both steadying and guiding the tool, while simultaneously exerting a slight pressure on the cutting edge. Both hands are braced against the stock and tool is pulled to the rear to make the cut. Depending on the grain of the wood, the scraper will cut best from only one direction. If the tool does not cut properly when pulled in one direction, reverse the stock in the vise and work from the opposite direction.

Often, changing the angle of the beveled cutting face of the tool will improve the way it cuts in certain woods, and like all cutting tools the edge must be sharpened from time to time to cut its best.

NOTE: The edge of a knife blade also makes an excellent scraper for the sides and corners of the magazine box mortice.

Figure 1-5

Figure 1-5 shows the No. 9, 5mm Swiss Carving gouge cutting the small radius in the magazine mortice. Both hands are braced against the stock and the fingers of the left hand not only position and guide the cutting edge of the chisel, but also exert rearward pressure against the tool. In the event of a slip, this rearward pressure prevents the tool from traveling too far forward and possibly damaging an adjacent area of inletting. This is called "Push-Pull" muscle control and is more fully explained in Figure 1-26.

Note the white lines drawn on the stock shown in Figure 1-5. With the metal in the wood a visual inspection revealed small gaps developing in these areas due to false spotting and the removal of too much wood. A white grease pencil was used as a reminder not to remove any more wood from these areas until inspection shows that the initial gaps have closed. Because most of the metal work of a rifle is either tapered or radiused, small gaps formed during the initial inletting will usually close up as the metal is inletted deeper into the wood.

INLETTING THE SEMI-INLETTED STOCK

Figure 1-6

In Figure 1-6 a small rawhide mallet is used to lightly tap the metal work into the wood. Use light taps only. If you force the metal in too deeply, the wedge shape of the magazine box may spread the wood apart too far and crack the stock.

As the inletting progresses, the amount of contact between the metal and wood increases, making the removal of the guard from the stock more difficult for each successive trial fitting. If the metal becomes stuck, the best way to loosen it is by alternately tapping the ends of the box from beneath, using a wooden dowel or brass drift passed upward through magazine box mortice and guard screw holes.

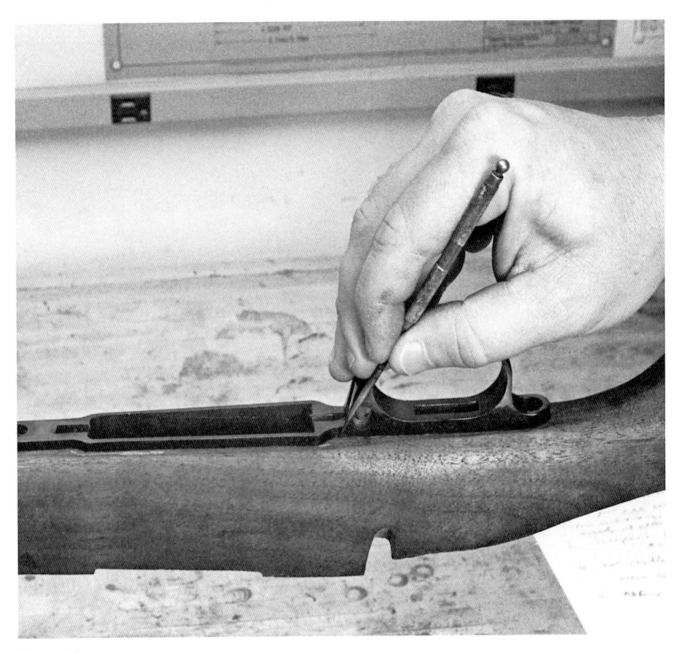

Figure 1-7

The metal projecting from the front and rear of the magazine box are called the tangs of the trigger guard. As each of these tangs makes contact with the surface of the wood, a scribe or sharp pencil is used to outline its position and shape onto the stock's surface.

Note that the front tang on a Mauser-type guard usually will contact the wood first. Trace and inlet it first, followed by the rear tang as it touches the stock.

At this stage of inletting the tangs must properly align with their respective pre-inletted mortices. If not, the misalignment must be corrected by removing wood from either the sides or corners of the magazine box mortice. If the front tang aligns properly, but the rear tang angles to one side, the rear tang may be bent. A quick check for this can be made by placing a square on the back of the magazine box. The sides of the trigger guard tang should be perpendicular to the back of the magazine box. If not, the rear tang must be straightened prior to inletting it into the wood.

The alignment of the trigger guard/magazine box tangs, and subsequent alignment of the front and rear guard screws, can affect the ultimate accuracy of the rifle. Ideally, the guard screws should be turned into the action at a true perpendicular to the bottom of the receiver, and the bottom of the screwheads should make full contact with the bottoms of the screwhead countersinks in the guard tangs. However, due to tolerances of the internal and external screw threads, and the large size of the threads, it is possible for the screws to seat into the receiver at a slight angle. When this happens, the receiver may be seated into the inletting with uneven tension on one side or the other, and the shoulders of the screws will make only partial contact with the bottoms of their countersinks.

This condition may result in a slight shifting of the action during recoil, or in nonrepeatable vibration patterns in the barrel due to the uneven stress on the action. As is well known, the barrel of a rifle vibrates like a violin string during firing with the muzzle proscribing a circular pattern of movement. For best accuracy, each bullet, shot after shot, must exit the muzzle at the same point on this circular path. Any uneven tension on the barrel or the action, or any shifting of the metal in the inletting will result in a different exit point from shot to shot and the concurrent loss of accuracy.

Figures 1-8

The wood between the lines traced around the tangs is removed using a 1-1/2-inch paring chisel for the straight sides (Figure 1-8) and a 1/4-inch in-cannel gouge for the inside radius at each end (Figure 1-9). If you have been careful to trace the exact outlines, you can safely remove the wood up to the inside of the lines (but not including the lines themselves). The reason we can do this without fear of leaving gaps in the finished inletting is that the sides of the tangs are beveled slightly and are narrower at the bottom than at the top. Since the narrower surface was touching the wood and was traced around, cutting to the lines, with full-depth cuts, simply delineates the narrower bottom dimensions of the tang at the bottom of the inletting mortice. Make the initial cuts straight down or slanted slightly inward. *Do not* undercut the wood here. The mortice will be cut to its finished width using the flat scraper shown in Figure 1-10.

Figure 1-9

The ends of the tangs are inletted by making a series of fine, overlapping cuts around the inside of the radius with the 1/4-inch in-cannel gouge as shown in Figure 1-9. Once again, make the initial cuts straight down. The inletting black from further trial fittings will show where final cuts need to be made. (See Figure 1-11 for instructions on the use of the 1/4-inch in-cannel gouge.)

Figure 1-10

In Figure 1-10 a flat scraper is used to finish inletting the sides of the trigger guard tang mortice. (Also review Figures 1-4 and 1-36, for further instructions on the use of the flat scrapers.)

Inletting the Semi-Inletted Stock

Figure 1-11

Figure 1-11 shows the 1/4-inch in-cannel gouge cutting an inside radius on a stock for a Sako barreled action. Note the size of the cut and that only the center of the tool's face is being used. When shaping an inside radius you should use a tool with a slightly shorter radius (i.e., having more curvature) than the radius to be cut. The radius is cut with a series of small overlapping cuts, removing only that wood indicated by the inletting black. Both hands are braced solidly against the stock and the thumb of the left hand steadies and positions the tool for each cut.

Figure 1-12

In Figure 1-12 a straight chisel is used for cutting the outside radius between the rear of the box and the trigger-guard tang. Outside radii are cut by using a series of very fine straight cuts walked around the perimeter of the radius. The fingers of the left hand both position and steady the tool for each cut.

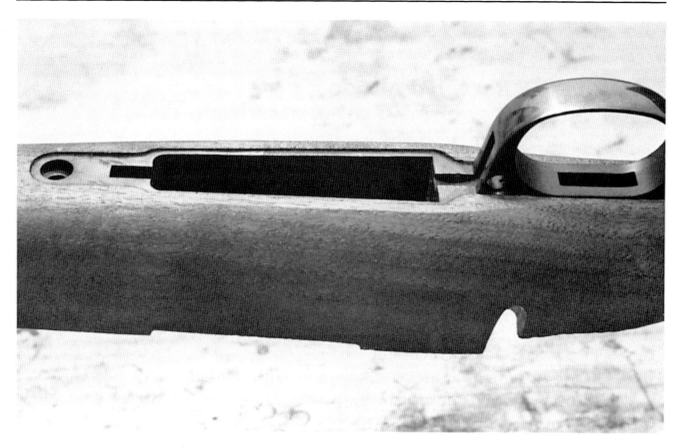

Figure 1-13

After several more trial fittings, the inletting is complete. The metalwork is even with or slightly below the surface of the wood. Bottoming tools and scrapers (See the Tool section) have been used to bring the metal and wood into full contact at the bottoms of the tang mortices. The front and rear of the magazine box fits snugly to help support the recoil abutment of the stock, and there are no major gaps in the inletting that require patching or repair.

NOTE: Mausers and Springfields require approximately 1/32-inch clearance between the top of the magazine box and the bottom of the action. Therefore, depending on the tolerances of the semi-inletted stock, the guard may eventually have to be inletted deeper, or metal removed from the top of the box in order to achieve the proper clearance.

For now, however, it is best to inlet the trigger guard even with, or slightly below the surface of the wood and move on to inletting the barreled action. After the barreled action is inletted, you can go back and inlet the trigger guard as needed to get the proper clearance between the guard and the bottom of the receiver.

Inletting the Barreled Action

SECTION-1-ROUGH INLETTING
Figures 1-14 through 1-32

If you are stocking a Mauser or other action that uses a one-piece trigger guard and magazine box (a one-piece guard), you already have inletted the guard and are now ready to proceed with inletting the barreled action. If, however, you are stocking a Sako or a Winchester Model 70, or any rifle that uses a two-piece trigger guard and magazine box, then the barreled action is inletted first, and the trigger guard inletted second. Also, if you are stocking a Model 70 or Sako, it might be helpful to review the information on tools, techniques, and inletting that are contained in the previous discussion on inletting the trigger guard before proceeding with the inletting of the barreled action.

The first step in inletting the barreled action into the semi-inletted stock is to install a pair of headless inletting guide screws. These screws replace the regular guard screws and help guide and position the action during the initial stages of the inletting.

The guide screws bend easily, however, and their alignment with the action should be checked frequently throughout the inletting process. This check should be made both visually and by using a small square placed against the bottom flat of the action.

With the guide screws in place, carefully align the barreled action with the pre-inletted stock mortices. In Figure 1-14, both the stock and the action have been leveled front to back and side to side. Note the bar stock support under the barrel, which helps to maintain the level front to back.

The leveling process shown here may or may not be possible, depending on the make of the barreled action. If the scope mount bases are used as a point of reference, they must be parallel to the bottom of the action and not canted to one side or the other. A quick check of the level of the bases can be made with a vernier caliper or an outside micrometer. Measure from the bottom flat of the action to each side of the base. Both measurements should be the same. Also, since the

Inletting the Semi-inletted Stock

Figure 1-14

jaws of the vernier are parallel, if they make full contact with both the top of the bases and the bottom of the action, the bases are square on the action. Suffice it to say, the closer that everything is to square at this point in the operation, the closer that initial outlining will be.

Figure 1-15

Once the barreled action has been leveled, its shape is outlined onto the top of the stock, as shown in Figure 1-15. Flatten one side of the pencil with a file or a belt sander. Place the flat side against the metal and tilt the pencil slightly to produce an outline that is slightly smaller than the actual size of the metal.

This outlining process is repeated several times during the course of the inletting, and as the metal sinks deeper into the wood we are able to get a more accurate outline by tilting the pencil progressively toward the vertical

Figure 1-16

each time an outline is made. These outlines are only a guide for the rough removal of wood. The edges of the final inletting are determined by the marks left by the inletting black.

In Figure 1-16, a small machinist's square is used to check the accuracy of the outline made in Figure 1-15. The square confirms that the pencil lines are inside the dimensions of the final inletting. As with the outlining, this check is only accurate if the metal is level and square with the stock. If the metal parts lean to one side or the other, neither the outlines nor the check will be valid.

Professional Stockmaking

Figure 1-17

In Figures 1-17 and 1-18, a pattern maker's template gauge is used to select the size and the shape of a chisel needed to make a particular cut. In use, the gauge is pushed against the metal work, and a chisel or scraper is chosen based on a direct comparison of the tool and the template.

Figure 1-18

As noted earlier, when cutting an inside radius you should use a tool with a slightly shorter radius (i.e., having more curvature) than the one that is to be cut. The final radius is shaped with a series of smaller overlapping cuts.

If you are using a semi-inletted stock with the barrel channel pre-inletted for either a factory barrel or an industry standard barrel contour, most of the work of inletting the barrel channel has already been done for you. (Review the materials in Figures 1-19 through 1-32 for information and instruction on the use of the various tools discussed therein and then proceed to Figure 1-33.)

If, however, you are using a custom, or nonstandard barrel contour, the stock must be ordered with the 1/2-inch guide channel, which leaves it up to the stockmaker to remove the bulk of the wood in the barrel channel.

The stock illustrated in Figure 1-19 was ordered with a 1/2-inch barrel channel and in this instance the bulk of the wood was removed with a No. 8 Swiss carving gouge and mallet. The mallet propels the gouge through the wood with a series of repeated light taps, actually allowing the tool to be steered in any desired direction. In use, the left hand is braced against the top of the stock with the muscles of the forearm exerting a slight backward cushioning force against the tapping of the mallet. The depth of the cut is controlled by the angle of the gouge in relation to the wood. The upper arm of the hand holding the mallet is pulled in tight against the body and all of the force necessary for these light, tapping blows is delivered with the forearm and wrist.

Once the bulk of the wood has been removed using the mallet and gouge, the mortice is deepened and widened with the 5/8-inch in-cannel gouge (barrel channel gouge) as shown in Figures 1-26 through 1-32 and finish inletted with the scrapers discussed in Figures 1-45 through 1-47.

Most wood cuts better with the grain. However, in this particular stock the grain ran uphill and crosswise at the end of the blank and cut better from front to back in this section of the channel.

NOTE: If the wood in the barrel channel cuts cleanly with either the No. 8 or in-cannel gouges, proceed to Figure 1-26. However, if the wood in the channel won't cut cleanly with the various gouges, but tends to tear or pop out chunks, alternative methods of rough inletting the barrel channel are shown in Figures 1-22 through 1-25.

INLETTING THE SEMI-INLETTED STOCK

Figure 1-19

Figure 1-20

Even though a light cut was being taken, the combination of a brash (brittle) piece of wood and an unseen curl in the grain structure caused a section of wood to pop out a full 1/8-inch in front of the chisel. Look closely at the size of the curl of wood at the front of the chisel. A long thin cut was being made when the wood popped. When a piece pops like this it is best to glue the piece back in place immediately as shown in Figure 1-21.

INLETTING THE SEMI-INLETTED STOCK

Figure 1-21

In Figure 1-21, a dowel rod was wrapped with tape to approximate the diameter of the barrel channel. Both surfaces of the tear were coated with white glue and a C-clamp was used to direct the pressure to the proper area. This setup applies even pressure to the glue joint and results in an invisible repair that is actually stronger than the surrounding wood.

Murphy's Law says that anything that can go wrong will go wrong, and this certainly applies to stockmaking. Mistakes happen, and a large part of being a stockmaker is learning how to fix these mistakes. Don't get mad and throw the chisel against the wall or kick the dog or kids. The chisel will have to be resharpened, the dog would be justified for biting your leg off, and the kids may grow up to be bigger than you are. The best thing to do when you make a mistake is to repair the damage and try to learn from it.

 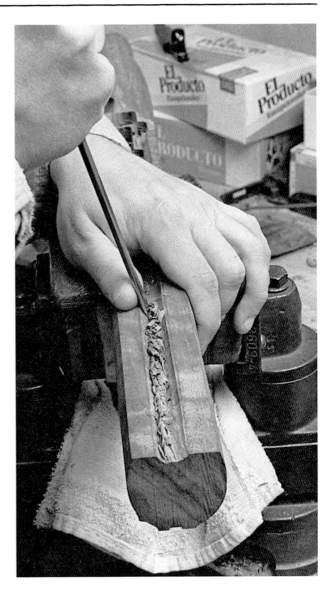

Figure 1-22 *Figure 1-23*

The fastest and easiest way to remove the excess wood from the barrel channel of the stock is to use the No. 8 gouge and the in-cannel gouges. (See Figures 1-19 and Figures 1-26 through 1-32.) However, if the wood refuses to cut cleanly with these chisels, there are several alternative methods for removal of this wood.

In Figures 1-22 and 1-23, a No. 5 or a No. 7 sweep chisel is held vertically in one hand while the thumb of the other hand positions and braces the tool for the cut. While pushing the tool downward, rotate the handle backward using the thumb as a fulcrum to cut a small arch of wood from the side of the channel. Overlap these cuts slightly up and down both sides of the

Figure 1-24

channel as shown in Figures 1-22 and 1-23. The ridges left at the bottom of the channel are removed with a spoon chisel, Figure 1-24, or with a barrel channel rasp, Figure 1-25.

An alternative tool for inletting the barrel channel in wood that won't cut cleanly with the gouges is the barrel channel rasp Figure 1-25. This is a treacherous little tool that must be used very carefully, as many an otherwise good inletting job has been ruined when the leading or trailing edge of the rasp wiped out an area on one side of the channel while the stockmaker was paying attention to another portion of the tool. In addition, if this tool rides up and rounds over the top edge of the inletting, it will create a gap between the metal and wood which can only be fixed by planing off the top of the stock and inletting the entire barrel and action deeper into the wood.

Never use this tool closer than about 0.020 inch to the final edge or depth of the channel. Rasps, by their very nature, tear and compress wood. This compression extends quite a way beneath the surface of the wood and must be completely removed from the barrel channel by either cutting or scraping. If these areas of compression are not removed completely, the first time the stock gets wet (or maybe the tenth time in the middle of a hunt) the areas of the compressed wood in the barrel channel may raise up and bear against the barrel causing a change in the rifle's zero.

On some woods, however, the rasp is the only tool that will do the job of removing the bulk of the wood from the channel. Use it, but be careful. The fingers of the left hand position and hold the rasp in the channel. The cutting stroke is a straight forward motion with the wrists in a semi-locked position and the forearms moving parallel to the plane of the work.

NOTE: Like the file, a rasp only cuts on the forward stroke. If you drag the teeth backward across the wood you will dull the rasp. To avoid this, lift the rasp slightly from the wood when drawing the tool back in preparation for the next forward stroke.

After having been rough-shaped and inletted with the barrel-channel rasp, the barrel channel is then finish inletted to full depth and width with the scrapers shown in Figures 1-45 through 1-47.

Figure 1-25

Rough Inletting the Barrel Channel with the In-cannel Gouges

Figures 1-26 through 1-32

As was noted in Figure 1-19, the fastest and easiest way to rough inlet an undersize barrel channel is to use the number 8 Swiss carving gouge and mallet followed by the in-cannel gouges. Figures 1-26 through 1-32 illustrate the use of the in-cannel gouges.

A push/pull muscle control is used when cutting with chisels to prevent a slipped tool from traveling too far forward and damaging another area of the inletting. To better understand push/pull muscle control, place your forearm perpendicular to your body and push outward against a table or a wall. Now tighten all of the other muscles in your shoulders and chest. These are the push/pull muscle groups working to oppose each other. In effect, by partially tightening these muscle groups in advance, you are preparing them to halt the forward movement of the chisel in case of a slip.

In general, when making heavy cuts with an in-cannel gouge, the center of the face of the chisel is used and the palm of the braced left hand both steadies and guides the tool. When making very fine cuts, the outer edges of the chisel are used for the cut and a tight grip finger position is used to guide and position the tool.

The channel is finish inletted to its full depth, one-half the diameter of the barrel, with the scrapers illustrated in Figures 1-45 through 1-47. A check for this one-half depth measurement is shown in Figure 1-48.

INLETTING THE SEMI-INLETTED STOCK

Figure 1-26

Figures 1-26 through 1-30, show the various hand positions used to control the in-cannel gouge when inletting the rear portion of the barrel channel. The chisel is pushed forward with the right hand, while the fingers and palm of the braced left hand guide and position the cutting face of the tool.

Figure 1-27

Inletting the Semi-inletted Stock

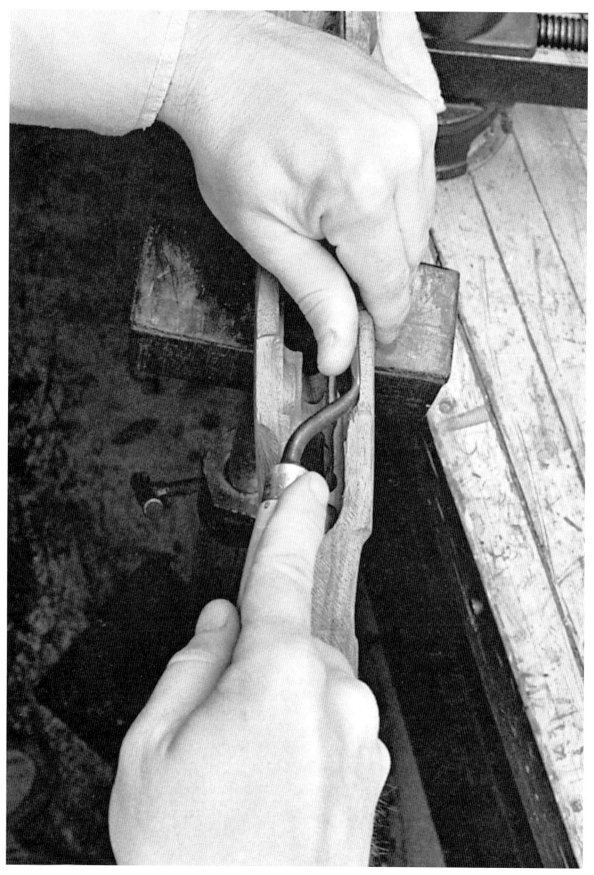

Figure 1-28

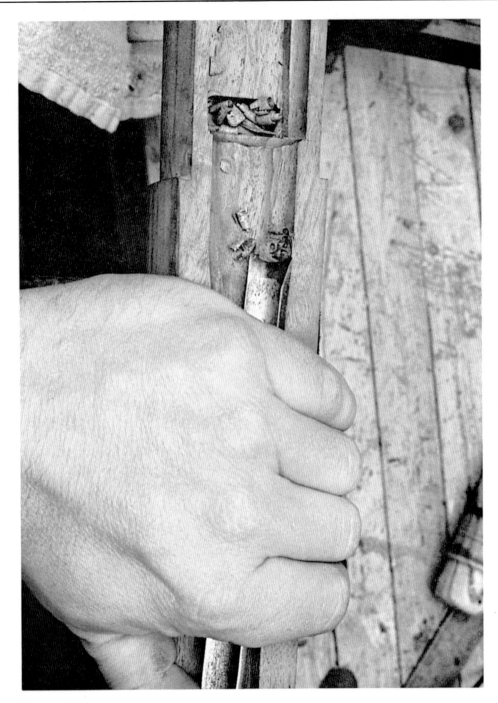

Figure 1-29

Figures 1-29 and 1-30 show the in-cannel gouge roughing in the taper between the barrel shank and the straight taper of the barrel. Because the inletting for this taper is sloped upward from the back to the front, it must be cut in from the front toward the back as shown. Note that the chisel rides in the crease between the fingers and the palm, and that the left hand is braced against the top and side of the stock.

Inletting the Semi-inletted Stock

Figure 1-30

Professional Stockmaking

Figure 1-31

Figures 1-31 and 1-32 show the tight grip finger position for guiding the in-cannel gouge along the top edges of the inletting. In this position the fingers of the left hand pull the tool against the side of the channel to steady and guide the face of the tool allowing very fine and precise cuts to be made.

Figure 1-32

Inletting the Barreled Action Semi-inlet
SECTION-2-FINISH INLETTING

Once the barrel channel has been roughed in, we are ready to fit the barreled action into the wood.

Install the inletting guide screws and lightly coat the barreled action with inletting black. Suffice it to say that the thinner the coating of inletting black on the metal, the easier it is to get an exact fit between the metal and the wood.

With the stock held in a vise by the forearm and the "third leg" supporting the bottom of the stock, carefully lower the barreled action into the wood. When the action has settled as far into the wood as it will on its own, give it a light tap with the rawhide mallet, as shown in Figure 1-33. A word of caution is in order here. A light tap is all that is necessary to get an accurate transfer of inletting black. If you use too heavy a blow, or try to force the barreled action in too deeply at one time, the curved sidewalls of the action and barrel will force the wood apart, and may crack the stock.

Carefully remove the barreled action from the stock and take note of the areas of contact as shown by transfer of inletting black. (Initially the metal work can be removed by hooking your finger through the bolt race in the rear receiver bridge and grasping the barrel in front of the forend tip, and lifting straight up. As the action sinks deeper into the inletting and makes greater contact with the wood, it becomes harder to remove. Light taps with the rawhide mallet on the underside of the front inletting guide screw will help unstick a stubborn action, which can then be lifted out by hand.) Note: Any rocking side to side or back and forth of the barreled action during either the insertion or removal from the stock will result in the false transfer of the inletting black from the metal to the wood. Removing too much wood at these points of false contact will result in gaps between the metal and the wood in the finished inletting. The sides and front radii of the receiver ring are the two worst areas for false marking to occur when inletting the barreled action. Remove wood carefully in these areas. Also, before removing

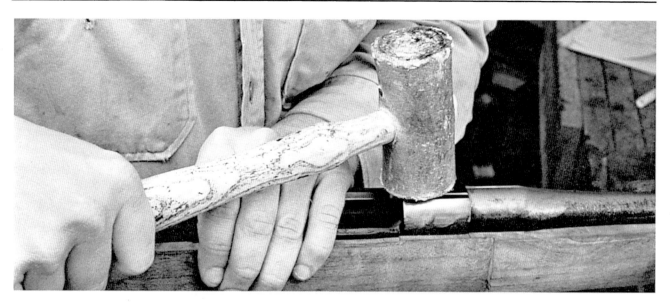
Figure 1-33

the barreled action from the stock make a visual check for gaps between the metal and the wood. Make a mark beside any gaps as a reminder not to remove more wood from those areas until the gaps close up.

During the first two or three trial fittings of the barreled action into the rough inletted stock, only a few points of contact (shown by the transfer of inletting black from the metal to the wood) will be noted. A chisel or scraper is then used to remove a small amount of wood at each of these contact points. The existing inletting black on the barreled action is brushed out and the action is again trial fitted into the stock and the wood is removed from additional points of contact. This process may have to be repeated 30 to 50 times before the barreled action is finally inletted to its full depth. Be patient and remove the wood slowly. The idea is to get as close a fit as possible between the metal and the wood.

One final thought before we get to the actual inletting of the barreled action. During inletting, examine the metal each time it is removed from the stock. Note the size and shape of those areas where the inletting black has scraped off the metal. Often this will give a better indication of the amount of contact between the metal and wood than by just examining the amount of inletting black deposited on the wood alone. This is especially true at the top edge of the inletting where the curved sides of the barrel and action spread the wood outward as they are forced down into the stock and leave only a thin line of inletting black at the edge of the wood.

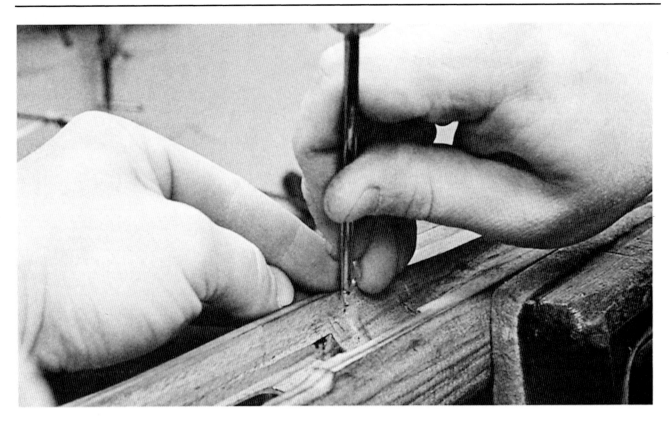

Figure 1-34

In Figure 1-34 a No. 9 sweep gouge is used to inlet the front radius of the receiver ring on a stock for a Model 1898 Mauser. This is generally one of the first points of contact the barreled action makes with the precut inletting mortices. Care should be taken to remove only minimal amounts of wood here as this area is prone to false markings during the insertion and removal of the barreled action from the stock. Because the sides of the barrel and action are radiused, small gaps along the sides of the receiver and barrel channel will generally close up as the metal is inletted deeper into the wood. However, since the front of the receiver is vertical, and has no expanding radii to fill small gaps, any gap in this area of the inletting will likely show in the finished inletting.

Very little pressure is needed for small cuts like this. Note that both hands are braced against the stock and that the fingers of the left hand are used to guide the placement of the chisel for a more accurate cut.

A No. 9 sweep gouge is used for this cut on the Mauser action. A 1/4-inch straight chisel is used for this cut on Model 70 Winchesters, Sakos, and similar actions having a flat face on the front of the receiver.

Inletting the Semi-inletted Stock

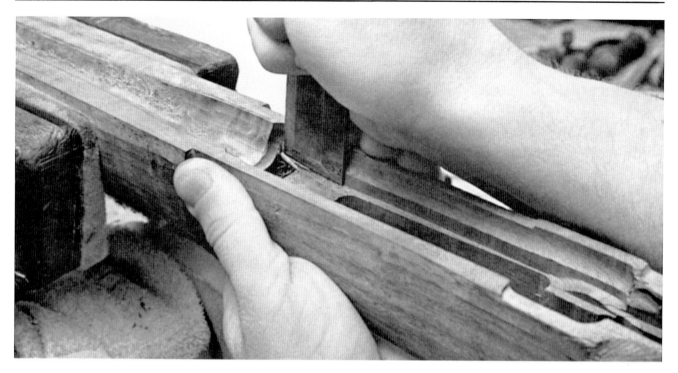

Figure 1-35

In Figure 1-35 a 1-1/2-inch straight chisel is used to cut the straight side wall inletting on a Sako action. The pre-existing inletting is used as a guide. The rear edge of the chisel is placed at the juncture of the side and bottom cuts of the inletting. The chisel is then rotated forward and the front portion of the blade shears a small shaving of wood from the side of the mortice. Note the tight, close-in grip on the chisel and that the fingers of the braced left hand are used to guide and position the chisel for the cut. The wider blade of this chisel makes it easier to continue the straight side of the pre-existing inletting. (NOTE: Sako and Model 70 Winchesters have a straight side wall on the lower receiver which is rough inletted as shown here. Mauser actions have a curved side wall, however, and this area is best "scraped in" using a flat scraper.)

A word of caution concerning Figure 1-35. Although the positioning of the left hand is safe here, on a cut made farther to the rear the chisel could slip through the magazine mortice resulting in a severe cut to the worker's left hand. The short gripping on the tool will help to prevent this, but it may be better to position the fingers of the left hand from left to right (across the top of the inletting) to guide the chisel for this particular cut. Think ahead. Note where a slipped chisel or other tool will come to rest, and keep your hands and fingers out of those places.

Figure 1-36 illustrates the use of the flat scraper in inletting the vertical lower side walls of the Sako and Model 70 Winchester receivers.

Scrapers remove very small, highly controlled shavings of wood from the inletting and are most valuable toward the end of the inletting where we must remove shavings only several thousandths of an inch thick to achieve a perfect fit between the metal and the wood. Note the curls of wood being removed in Figure 1-36. In order to remove curls such as this, the scraper must be kept sharp, and generally will cut most efficiently when used to cut with the grain of the wood.

Use both hands to guide and position the scraper. Pull the tool straight back, with the wrists and forearms of both arms in a semi-locked position and moving both in the same plane as the desired cut.

The use of the flat scraper was discussed in the section dealing with the inletting of the Mauser trigger guard/magazine box. If you are stocking a Mauser or Springfield you are already familiar with the use of this tool. If you are stocking a Model 70 or a Sako, where the barreled action is inletted before the trigger guard, you may want to read the information contained in Figure 1-4 for further instructions on the use of this tool.

Inletting the Semi-inletted Stock

Figure 1-36

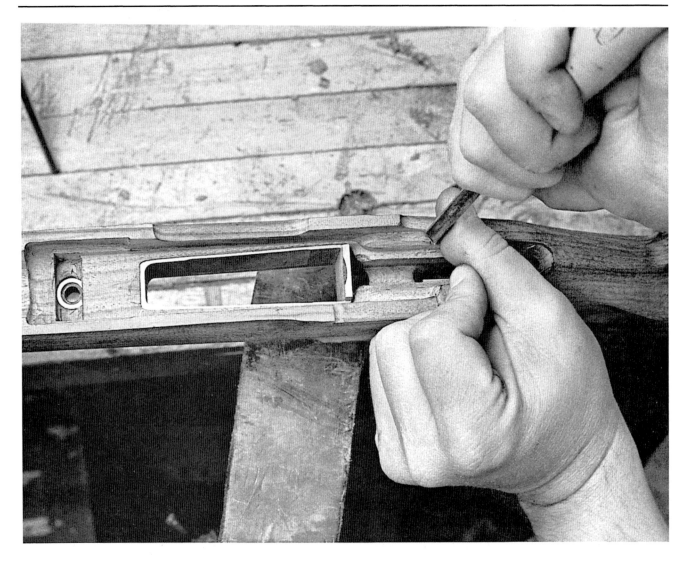

Figure 1-37

Inletting the Rear of the Receiver

Figures 1-37 and 1-38

The size and shape of the transition between the rear of the receiver and the tang varies from one action type to another. On a Mauser, it forms a wide radius cut and is inletted with the in-cannel gouge shown in Figure 1-37. (Note that both hands are braced against the stock and that the fingers of each hand are used to position the tool and guide the cut.) On the Sako, this cut is almost square and is inletted as shown in Figure 1-38. On a Winchester Model 70 this area is simply an extension of the side wall of the receiver and is inletted with a No. 5 sweep gouge followed by the Fisher inletting scrapers Figures 1-45 and 1-46.

Figure 1-38

In Figure 1-38 a deep mortice chisel is used to cut the square corner between the rear of the receiver and the tang on a Sako action. Although this may appear to be an awfully large chisel for making this small cut, the weight of the tool is an asset here. All of the necessary cutting force comes from the weight of the tool and the downward push of the thumb and first two fingers of the right hand. This allows the stockmaker to concentrate only on the cut itself, and not worry about supplying a lot of the force to make the cut. (NOTE: cutting across "end grain" as illustrated here requires a razor-sharp chisel. If, instead of cutting cleanly, the wood tends to tear and compress, your chisel is too dull and needs to be resharpened.)

Inletting the Sides of the Tang

Figure 1-39

Mauser and Sako actions have straight rear tangs that are slightly beveled from the top to the bottom. This bevel makes the inletting of the tang easier because the metal becomes wider as it is inletted deeper into the wood and any small gaps along the top edge of the inletting will most likely close up by the time the metal has been inletted to its full depth.

As the inletting progresses and the bottom of the tang makes contact with the stock, a sharp pencil or scribe is used to transfer the shape of the tang onto the top of the stock. A straight chisel is then used to cut straight down to the bottom of the mortice along the lines marked on the stock. In Figure 1-39 a 1-1/2-inch straight chisel is used to rough inlet the tang inletting on a Mauser action. In this instance the pre-existing inletting was close to the finish dimensions at the rear of the mortice, but not at the front. The rear corner of the chisel was placed at the bottom of the existing mortice and the blade then rotated forward and downward several times. Each cut removed a thin slice of wood. The thumb of the left hand both positions and guides the tool for each successive cut.

After the bulk of the wood on the side of the tang is removed in this manner, the inletting is finished with a flat scraper using the inletting black to show where wood needs to be removed.

If you are stocking a Model 70, the straight section on the bottom of the tang is cut in with a wide, straight chisel. Since the upper portion of the tang is an extension of the sides of the action, it is rough inletted with either the in-cannel gouge or the No. 5 sweep gouge and then finish — inletted with the Fisher inletting scrapers as discussed in Figures 1-45 and 1-46.

Inletting the Semi-inletted Stock

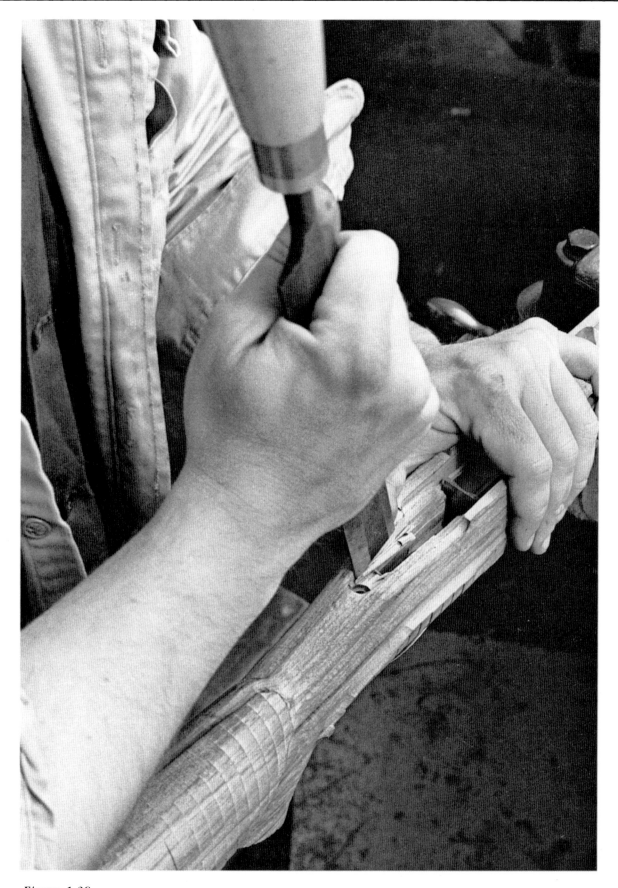

Figure 1-39

Inletting the Curved Sides of the Receiver
Figure 1-40

In Figure 1-40 a 5/8-inch in-cannel gouge is used to rough in the side radius of a receiver. Since this was a roughing cut (note the pencil outline visible just to the side and front of the chisel), we were able to take out quite a long, thin curl of wood. The actual curl measured almost three inches long, and wasn't quite .020-inch thick. Note the braced left hand and tight finger grip, used to control, guide, and steady the chisel. (See Figures 1-26 through 1-32 for further instruction on the use of this tool.) This chisel is used for the roughing in of the curved sides of the receiver and also (after its use has been mastered) for the finishing cuts. However, until you are totally comfortable with making controlled cuts of 0.004 inch or less with this tool, the final inletting is best done with either the Fisher inletting scraper or the barrel channel scraper (see Figures 1-45 through 1-47).

Inletting the Semi-inletted Stock

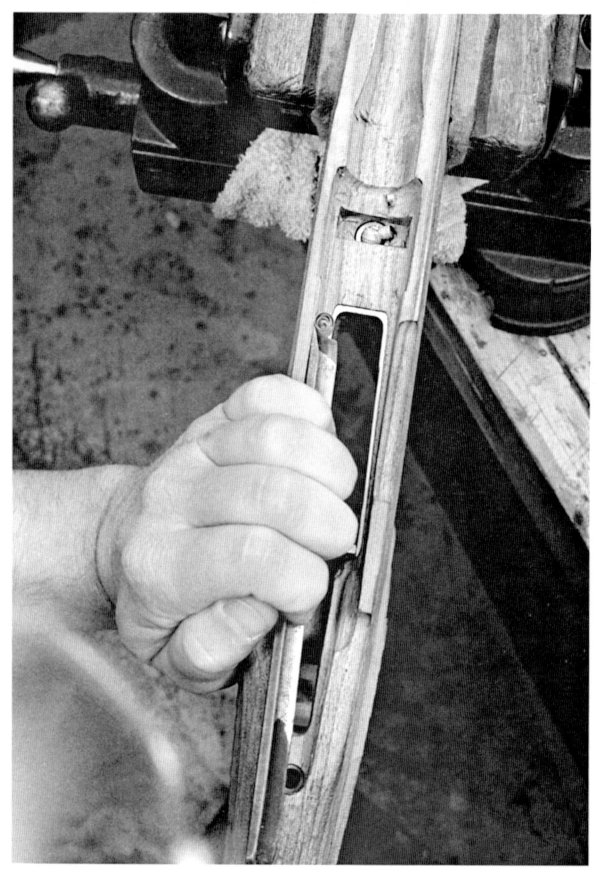

Figure 1-40

Inletting the Recoil Lug Mortice
Figures 1-41 and 1-42

Once the action has started to settle into the stock, the bottom surface of the recoil lug will make contact with the wood. The transfer of the inletting black will delineate the front, back, and sides of the recoil lug mortice. The front, sides, and bottom of the recoil lug should not make contact with the mortice in the finished inletting. These areas are relieved slightly during the course of the inletting.

In most instances, the corners of the pre-cut mortice will be radiused. A 1/4-inch straight chisel (Figure 1-41) is used to square out the corners of the pre-existing mortice. The fingers of the braced hands are used to both guide and to provide the cutting force to the chisel for these light cuts.

An alternative method is used when a heavier cut is desired or necessary. The chisel is gripped higher up and the thumb of the left hand guides and positions the cut. The force necessary for the cut comes from a straight, downward movement of the right hand.

In Figure 1-42, a 1-inch straight chisel is used to cut in the back face of the recoil lug mortice. This area should only be cut in after its exact position has been determined by the inletting black. Full contact between the recoil lug and the rear of the recoil lug mortice is vital to the structural integrity of the stock. Once this surface shows full contact with the recoil lug, as shown through the transfer of inletting black, do not remove any more wood. If, for whatever reason, too much wood is removed, you can repair the damage by either gluing in a wooden filler and then re-inletting the recoil lug, or by using a small amount of glass bedding to fill the void. (NOTE: I have on occasion inletted a steel plate into the recoil lug mortice, but the positioning and inletting of such a plate can be complicated. It is better for the beginning stockmaker to correct any error either by replacing the wood or by glass bedding this area should too much wood be removed.)

Inletting the Semi-inletted Stock

Figure 1-41

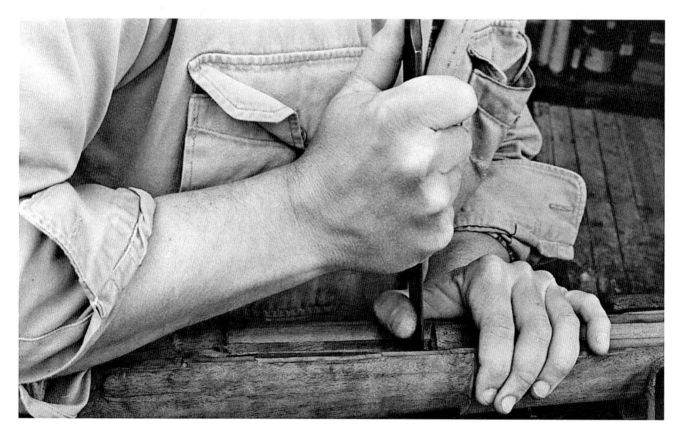

Figure 1-42

Professional Stockmaking

Figure 1-43

Figure 1-43 shows the use of the 1/4-inch in-cannel gouge for inletting the radius at the rear of the tang. The thumb of the left hand positions and guides the chisel in a series of small overlapping cuts as indicated by the inletting black. NOTE: To prevent possible damage to the stock from the barreled action moving backward on the initial firing, the wood directly behind the tang should be relieved slightly before firing the rifle for the first time.

Inletting the Semi-inletted Stock

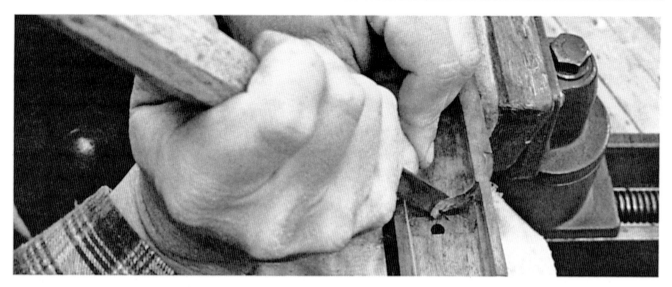

Figure 1-44

Inletting the Lower Section of the Receiver Ring Radius

Figure 1-44

In Figure 1-44, a No. 7 sweep gouge is used to rough in the radius at the bottom of the receiver ring on a Sako action. Both hands are braced against the stock, and the thumb of the left hand is used to both position the tool and as a pivot against which the tool is rotated. The right hand provides the cutting force for the tool and moves downward and backward with a slight twist of the wrist to present the face of the chisel as needed to match the contour of the required mortice.

On the Mauser action the lower portion of the receiver ring radius is inletted with a No. 9 sweep gouge. For this cut the right hand again rotates downward and backward with a slight twisting motion of the wrist to help the chisel cut the wood at the very bottom of the mortice.

Never brace or pivot the tool against the top edge of the inletting. Doing so will result in a small dent at each pivot or brace point that may appear as a gap in the finished inletting. Dents can often be steamed out using a hot iron and a damp cloth. The steam causes compressed fibers in the wood to expand back and to their original shape. If the wood fibers are broken however, steaming will not restore the wood to its original shape. Place a damp rag over the dent and let it sit overnight. The broken fibers may absorb enough water to re-expand to their original shape.

Figure 1-45

Using the Fisher Inletting Scrapers in the Barrel Channel
Figures 1-45 and 1-46

Figures 1-45 and 1-46 illustrate the use of the Fisher inletting scrapers in the barrel channel of the stock. In use, both hands are braced and slide along the stock with the tool. Most of the cutting force comes from either the thumb (Figure 1-45) or forefinger (Figure 1-46), depending on the direction of the cut. The off hand controls the tilt of the blade and determines the cutting face of the tool presented to the work. As with most scrapers, these tools work best when there is a slight angle between the cutting face of the tool and the wood, which allows you to cut curves of different radii with the same tool.

Fisher inletting scrapers are sold in sets of two scrapers, each scraper having two different radii. The larger scrapers are used for scraping both the barrel channel and the curved side walls of the receiver inletting.

INLETTING THE SEMI-INLETTED STOCK

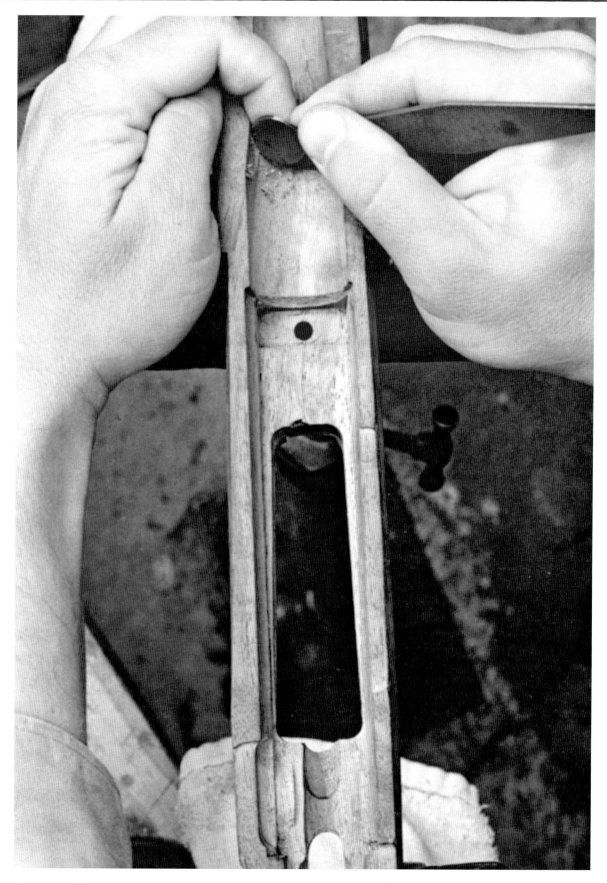

Figure 1-46

Using the Barrel Channel Scraper

Figure 1-47

In Figure 1-47, a barrel channel scraper is used for the final inletting and smoothing of the barrel channel. The same warnings apply to the use of this tool as applied to use of the barrel channel rasp (see Figure 1-25). More than one stock job has been ruined with this tool by having either the leading or trailing edge ride up over the top (sharp) edge of the inletting, or wipe out the off side of the mortice while the stockmaker was watching the center of the tool.

This scraper, along with the Fisher scrapers described earlier, is also used for the final inletting of the curved sides of most action mortices. It will cut on either the pull or push stroke. The worker's forearms and wrists are in a semi-locked position and move parallel to the plane of the work.

Because of this tool's circular shape, quick cutting ability, and the clean cuts it leaves, it is often the tool of choice for deepening the barrel channel to its full depth (one-half the diameter of the barrel at each point along the length of the barrel). It is an excellent tool for making longer, curved cuts. The multi-blade design of this tool makes it especially useful in stocks that have alternating areas of hard and soft wood, or fiddleback grain patterns where a single-blade tool tends to dig into the softer areas and skim over harder ones leaving an uneven surface to the inletting.

This tool is available in several different sizes. The 1/2-, 9/16-, and 5/8-inch tools are the ones most often used in stockmaking.

INLETTING THE SEMI-INLETTED STOCK

Figure 1-47

Determining Half Depth of the Barrel Channel
Figure 1-48

The easiest way to determine if the barrel channel is at half depth is to place a small machinist's square in the channel and then check the points at which the legs and point of the square contact the edges of the channel. If both legs and the point of the square touch the wood, the channel is half its width deep. If only one leg and the point touch the bottom of the channel, the channel needs to be deeper. If the point of the square doesn't reach the bottom of the channel, but both legs of the square contact the sides of the channel, the channel is either too deep or not wide enough. (This check is easier to make than to describe.) To recap, however, if both legs of the square touch the top edge of the inletting and the corner of the square contacts all points on the sides or bottom of the channel as the square is rotated, the barrel channel is round and half as deep as it is wide.

One final thought concerning finish inletting of the barrel channel. Because most sporting rifle barrels taper from the breech to the muzzle, the diameter of the barrel changes continually. It is virtually impossible, given the tools that are available, to have an exact and full contact between the wood and the metal at every point along the channel, nor is it necessarily desirable.

Each rifle barrel is a separate entity unto its own. The accuracy potential of any barrel can only be determined by a trial and error search of the variables concerning accuracy, changing only one variable at a time. These variables include, but are not exclusive to, a correctly bedded action which is free of any induced stress and that does not shift from shot to shot, choice of ammunition either factory or hand loaded, the individual shooter's agility to shoot from a benchrest, and lastly a barrel that has been inletted into the stock without any induced stresses at any point on its sides or bottom surfaces. Some barrels will shoot best fully free floated, others shoot best with a slight upward pressure at the tip of the forearm, and still others shoot best fully bedded. Which type of bedding you eventually use can only be determined by test firing

Figure 1-48

the rifle at the range. In general, if your rifle strings shots horizontally, there is uneven pressure along one side of the barrel channel. Vertical stringing may be caused by too much or too little upward pressure at the end of the forearm. Shots that group in a three-shot/two-shot pattern generally indicate problems with the action bedding, which allow the action to shift from shot to shot. Groups that scatter all over the paper can be caused by any number of reasons, including an improperly bedded action, loose action or scope mount and base screws, or improper ammunition (try a different brand or change your reloads).

We have gotten away from the task at hand here — the finish inletting of the barrel channel. What we want initially is to fit the sides of the barrel channel as closely as possible to the barrel without any sideways stresses and perhaps with a small amount of upward pressure at the end of the forearm.

Inletting the Curved Sidewalls of the Receiver
Figure 1-49

In Figure 1-49, the curved sidewalls of the Sako action are inletted with the barrel channel scraper. This tool, along with the Fisher scraper, is used for the finish inletting cuts along the upper radius of Mauser, Sako, Winchester Model 70, and Springfield receivers.

As noted in Figure 1-47, this tool must be used with care to prevent the rounding of the top edge of the inletting or damage to the adjacent areas of inletting.

INLETTING THE SEMI-INLETTED STOCK

Figure 1-49

Professional Stockmaking

Figure 1-50

Figure 1-51

Inletting Complete

Figures 1-50 and 1-51

Figures 1-50 and 1-51 show the completed inletting of a Sako barreled action in its stock. Note the sharp, smooth interior surfaces and the firm contact of the stock and the bottom of the receiver, as shown by the inletting black in Figure 1-50.

The top edge of the inletting shows good wood to metal fit. The actual contact between the metal and wood can be seen by the thin black line of inletting black visible on the edge of the barrel channel in Figure 1-50.

Although the above heading reads, "Inletting Complete," there are still several procedures to complete before the inletting is really finished. First, we must use steam to raise any hidden compressed areas of wood in the inletting. (Yes, I know that all of the tools we used for the finish inletting left a smooth surface. However, all through the inletting process we have been tapping the action into the wood with a rawhide mallet, and toward the end of the procedure we used T-handled stockmaker's screws to pull the action even more firmly into the wood. There exists, then, the distinct likelihood that somewhere along the line we have compressed the wood well below the now-clean surface. If that wood expands at some later date, it can cause problems. It is better to take care of those potential problems now before we seal the inletting than to have them crop up after the job seems to be done.)

The procedure is simple. Use the scrapers to lightly remove all traces of inletting black from the inletting. Next, lay a damp cloth over the top of the stock and use a clothes iron to apply heat to the cloth. The steam created will expand any compressed wood back to its original shape. The barreled action is then re-inserted into the stock and any areas that need the attention of the chisels and scrapers are shown by the inletting black.

Next, reassemble the rifle using the action screws to pull the metal down into the wood. Tighten both screws snugly and then set each screw by placing the blade of a well-fitting screwdriver into the slot and tapping the screwdriver with a mallet. This relieves the tension on the screw threads so that another one-quarter turn, or more, can be taken up. (NOTE: the Model 70 Winchester has three action screws. Use this method to tighten the front and rear screws only. The middle screw should only be tightened enough to hold the front of the guard bow into the wood. Accuracy problems will occur if the center screw is tightened too much.) Now, alternately loosen and tighten the action screws and look for any movement of the action or barrel. Any movement of the barreled action while loosening and tightening the action screws indicates a high spot in the inletting that must be taken care of before the final assembly of the rifle.

The last step is to take the rifle to the range and fire several rounds downrange. This settles the metal into its final position in the stock. This should be done before the now-ultra-thin coat of inletting black is removed from the metal. (Remember, we have tried not to add any inletting black since applying that first coat, but rather have brushed out that original coat all through the spotting-in process.) After firing, remove the metal from the stock and examine the points of contact indicated by the inletting black. The rear of the recoil lug mortice and the flats of the bottom of the action should show full contact at this stage. If so, and the accuracy of the completed rifle is acceptable, you are done. If not, now is the time to correct any problems.

Seal the inletting with either a commercial wood sealer or brush on several coats of thinned stock finish. To avoid any buildup of finish in the inletting, let the wood absorb all of the sealer that it can and then wipe out any excess.

Now, the inletting is complete.

Inletting the Semi-inletted Stock

50 caliber wildcat rifle. Note the crisp lines of the ejection port cut out.

Figure 2-1

Authors note: Of all of the photos in Book II, I have chosen the above as the best example of the book's subtitle — Through the Eyes of the Stockmaker. *In Figure 2-1, the crossing file is being used for the finish shaping and rounding of the pistolgrip of the stock.*

BOOK II

FINISH SHAPING THE STOCK
Introduction to Shaping

In the design and shaping of a stock the stockmaker must become many people. He becomes an engineer who understands the force vectors of recoil and how to minimize their effects on the perceived or felt recoil to the shooter. He becomes a tailor who gradually removes wood from various areas of the stock until a precise fit of the stock to the particular individual is achieved. Lastly, he becomes a sculptor who combines the lines that the engineer, the architect, and tailor specify into the flowing, harmonious, functional line form known as a gunstock.

Throughout the shaping and the sanding portions of the text there are photographs of stocks with white lines drawn on them. These lines indicate the direction, or flow, of the various shapes of the stock or the shapes of the transitions between adjacent areas. A ruler placed along any of the straight lines on the buttstock, the action, or along the fore-arm of the stock should be level, without any bumps or dips, the entire length of the line. The curved lines in the comb fluting, and on the wrist and the grip also indicate the shape much the same as the contour lines on a topographical map show shape. For our purpose these lines will be referred to as "flow lines." In addition, since the actual shape of the stock is made up of a series of flow lines, the term "line flow" will be used to mean shape. For example, if the text reads "The line flow of the lower buttstock tapers upward from the toe of the stock toward the wrist," this is saying that the "shape" of the lower buttstock tapers upward from the toe toward the wrist. Figure 2-2 illustrates the line flow diagrams of the stock.

The shaping of a stock is accomplished in stages. During the first stage, the rough shaping, the stock's profile lines are established and the stock is shaped to within 1/8" of its finished dimensions. All of the architectural features of the stock, major line flows, and shapes of the transitional areas between adjacent line flows, are located and roughed in. NOTE: shaping the stock slightly oversize during the rough shaping allows the stockmaker to fully develop the lines and shapes of the stock, while leaving sufficient extra wood to correct any minor mistakes or make any architectural changes during the final shaping of the stock.

The next stage in shaping is the finish shaping and detailing stage. During this stage of shaping the architectural features of the stock are refined and the last 1/8" of excess wood is removed from the outside of the stock, bringing the stock to its final form and dimensions. Unlike during the rough shaping of the stock where large amounts of wood are removed and the stockmaker is able to follow a progression of steps to shape each individual area, in the finish shaping only small amounts of wood are removed at any one time and the stockmaker must pay attention to the stock as a whole, working each area as needed until the entire stock slowly evolves into its final form.

The best advice that the author can give on the shaping of a stock is to work slowly and carefully. Follow the line flow diagrams in the text and use a proven straightedge to confirm that those lines that are suppose to be straight and level are indeed straight and level. Gradually shape each line flow and blend each into the adjacent line flows. Frequently check the lines of the stock by squinting down each from both ends of the stock. In order to see the overall line flow of the stock it is often helpful to step back and view the stock from a distance. Use your fingertips to feel for any unwanted bumps or dips in the curved areas of the stock. Try to make both sides of the stock symmetrical by first shaping an area on one side of the stock and then turning the stock over and shaping that same area on the other side. Use a pattern-maker's template gauge to confirm that both sides are the same. If you have problems developing a particular line flow, shape the lines on either side of the problem area, as this will often help the problem line fall into place. If this doesn't help, work on some other part of the stock for a while and come back to this area later. Nothing is more conducive to poor craftsmanship than the aggravation and exasperation of not knowing what to do in order to correct a problem. Charging straight ahead is the worst thing to do, as it will probably create even greater problems. At times like this it is best to walk away from the bench for a while and do something else. Everybody has good days and bad days. On the good days the tools work magic and do everything that you want them to do. On the bad days nothing seems to go right. If you find that you are having a bad day, do anything, wash the car, take a walk, go fishing - but don't work on stocks. The mistakes that you make will take far longer to fix than the hours you would have put in anyway. Besides, scouting for deer season or spending the day fishing is not an entirely bad way to spend your time.

In order to begin to appreciate and understand just how the flowing lines and curves of a graceful stock blend into the overall design of a rifle, the student of stockmaking must first study the lines and shapes of as many guns as possible. Go to the local or regional gun shows and handle the guns, noting not only what looks good but also what feels good about each. Look for rifles by the firms of Griffin and Howe, Sedgely, Hoffman Arms, or Kimber, and by individual makers such as the late Bob Owens and Leonard Brownwell or contemporary makers such as Greg Boeke, Mark Lee, Jerry Fisher, and Dale Goens among others. Look for any pre-war English or German bolt action sporters, for although these rifles were designed to be used with iron sights and by contemporary standards have combs that are too thin and too much drop at the heel, these stocks often exhibit highly refined line flow. Also, pay close attention to any original British muzzle loading rifles and shotguns. Many of the line forms and design features, as applied to the modern bolt action rifle stock, were conceptualized and highly refined in both form and function during the periods of muzzle loading rifles and shotguns.

That the successful stockmaker must first become a student of the design history of stocks is best exemplified by a quote from *Modern Gunsmithing* second edition 1933 by Clyde Baker. As Mr. Baker points out, the following was written as advice in a field far different from gunsmithing, however the words not only aptly apply to stockmaking but also to almost every endeavor, craft, or art form and are as true today as they were when they were written well over a half century ago.

"The best kind of originality is that which comes after a sound apprenticeship; that which shall prove to be sound blending of a firm conception of all useful precedent and the progressive tendencies of an open mind. For let a man be as able and original as he may, he cannot afford to discard knowledge of what has gone before or what is now going on in his own trade or profession. Art does not flourish in hidden places, nor under restraint, nor in ignorance of what talent and genius have accomplished and are now accomplishing throughout the world. For to follow precedent wisely does not mean to imitate slavishly one great exemplar, but to study all of the masters faithfully, letting their great achievements sink slowly into the mind in order that we may patiently derive from the richness of our acquired knowledge an organized system and attitude of our own. The sprightly minded young man, who with his first business breath projects the new and startling, inevitably becomes tiresome, and is driven to an early disappearance; while the slower, more solidly endowed student will at least spend as much of his time in avoiding mistakes as in evolving brilliant schemes wherewith to dazzle his contemporaries."

Lastly, a word about lighting is in order here. Quite simply, you have to be able to see the contours of a shape in order to form that shape. The best lighting that I have found for stock work is one of the swing arm lights available at hardware and office supply stores. In my shop this lamp is mounted on the wall behind my bench and about 18 inches higher than the bench top. Mounted as such the lamp is efficient to use and also out of the way of the work area. This lamp swings on an arm and the light can be directed to wherever it is needed. Swinging the lamp side to side or up and down allows the stockmaker to light even the smallest detail of the stock, and create the shadows and highlights needed to give the work a three dimensional quality which shows the contours of the area being worked on. A 60- or 75-watt bulb will provide all of the light needed

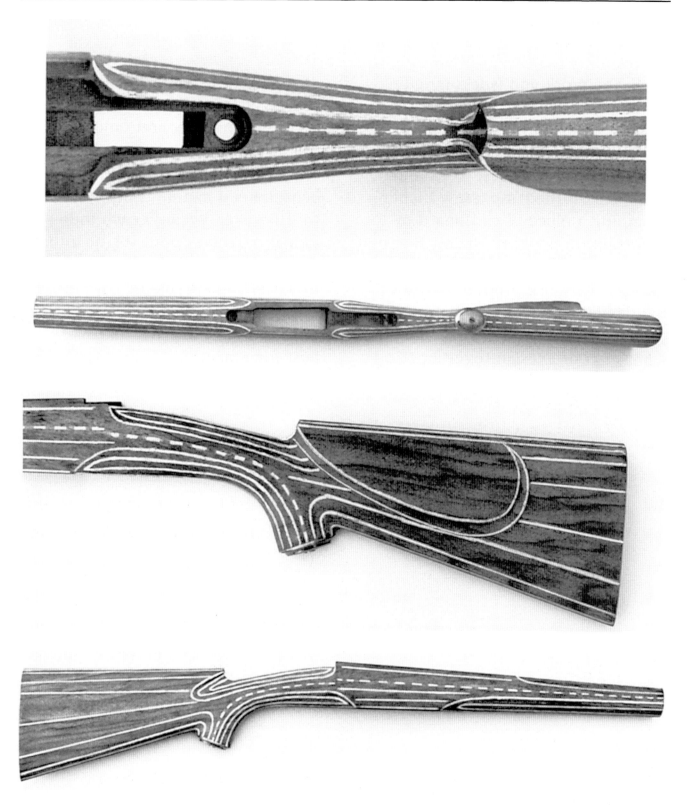

Figure 2-2

Figure 2-2 illustrates several line flow diagrams for the typical bolt action sporter stock.

to do the work and is less fatiguing on the eyes than the brighter bulbs. Because this lamp is positioned close to the work, and also to the worker's eyes, it is best to extend the shade of the lamp a few inches by taping a piece of cardboard or construction paper to the outside of the lamp shade. This will allow you to light the work properly without the danger of having the light shine directly into your eyes (which could damage your eyesight over a period of time.) In my shop this is the only source of light that I use for the inletting, shaping, and sanding of a stock. However, other stockmakers work well under overhead fluorescent lights. I cannot, but they seem to. However, because each individual perceives both the quantity and the quality of light differently, it is best to experiment with different types and intensities of lighting until you find the one that works best for you.

Finish Shaping the Stock

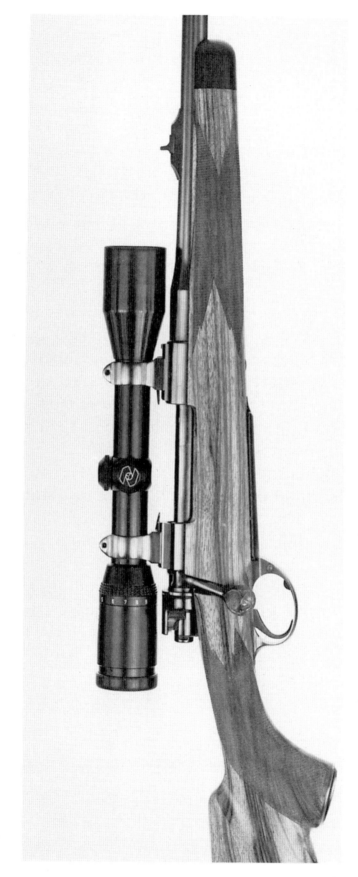

Zeiss Rifle - Caliber 280. Owner Col. Dick Kayser U.S.M.C. Used by Zeiss optical to display their scopes at the 1988 NRA convention.

Shaping the Stock

Section 1
Fitting the stock to the individual shooter
Figures 2-3 through 2-11

Perhaps the most important aspect of the efficient use of a rifle in the field is the tailoring of the stock dimensions to the specific physical characteristics of the individual. With a correctly fitted stock, no conscious effort is required to mount the rifle or position the head for correct sight alignment. The instant the butt settles into the shoulder, the cheek makes firm contact with the comb of the stock, the eye aligns with the sights and the shooting hand is correctly positioned on the grip for easy access to the trigger. A rifle so stocked has the handling qualities of a fine bird gun; it points where the shooter is looking, making the acquisition of game in the sights almost instantaneous upon shouldering the rifle. Faster, more frequent and accurate shots on game are the result.

Just as the physical characteristics of individuals vary from one person to another, so must the dimensions of the gunstock vary to accommodate each individual. The length of pull, amount of cast or toe, the drop at the heel and comb, and the positioning and circumference of the grip of a stock vary depending on the size, shape, and mounting technique of the individual shooter.

Figure 2-3 illustrates the layout and design of a stock being made from a square blank. If you are stocking from a semi-inletted stock however, and wish to fit the stock properly, you must order the stock turned oversize with plenty of extra wood through the buttstock and wrist.

Finish Shaping the Stock

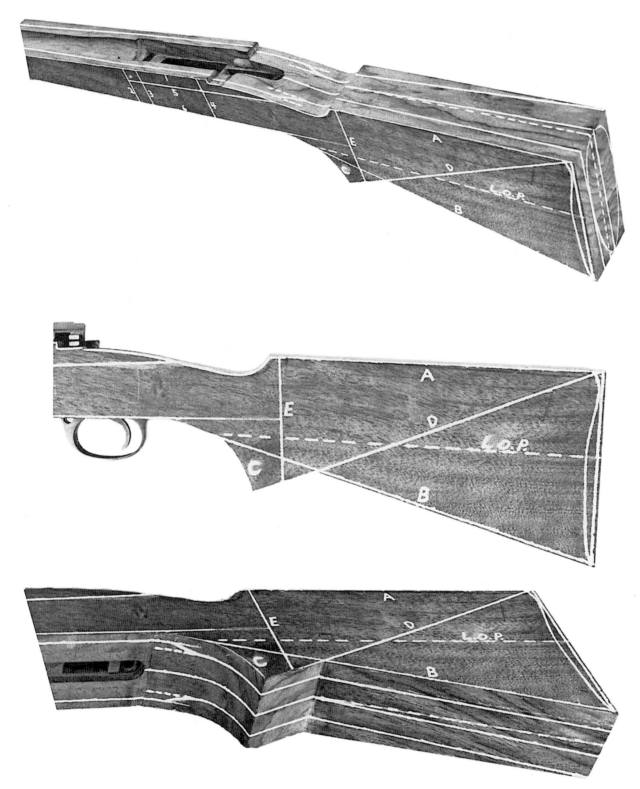

Figure 2-3

Figure 2-3 illustrates the number of dimensions that are required to correctly fit a rifle stock made from a square blank to an individual shooter. Each is discussed in the pages that follow.

Length of Pull

Figure 2-4

The length of pull (LOP) is the distance from the center of the trigger to the center of the buttplate. It is determined by the physical size of the shooter, the caliber of the rifle and the method the shooter uses to mount the rifle on his shoulder.

Shooters who throw the rifle forward as part of the initial movement to mount it, and then pull the rifle back into the shoulder, can use a slightly longer LOP than a shooter of the same physique who swings his rifle up, but not outward, as he shoulders it.

A slightly longer LOP is often used on large bore, heavy recoiling rifles. The longer pull allows the shooter to stock crawl with his head and neck and puts his shoulder at a full rearward position ready to accept the recoil. A shooter thus braced is able to "roll with the punch" and receives less felt, or perceived, recoil than the shooter whose head snaps forward and his shoulder backward as the rifle is fired.

The best way to determine an individual's LOP is to mount a rifle that is known to be too long, and then progressively shorten the stock until the rifle can be shouldered comfortably. If a recoil pad is to be fitted there is an added margin of safety in determining the correct length, for the thickness of the pad will be cut off of the stock at some later time. If a steel buttplate is to be fitted, the margin for error is small and, in addition, sufficient extra wood must be left to properly inlet the buttplate. To achieve the best fit, hunting clothes should be worn while determining the length of pull.

Before going on, consider that the length of pull may be affected by the pitch of the stock in that an incorrectly pitched stock may cause the stock maker to set the LOP too long or too short. It is therefore advised that you read through this entire section on stock fitting prior to removing any wood from the butt of the stock.

Finish Shaping the Stock

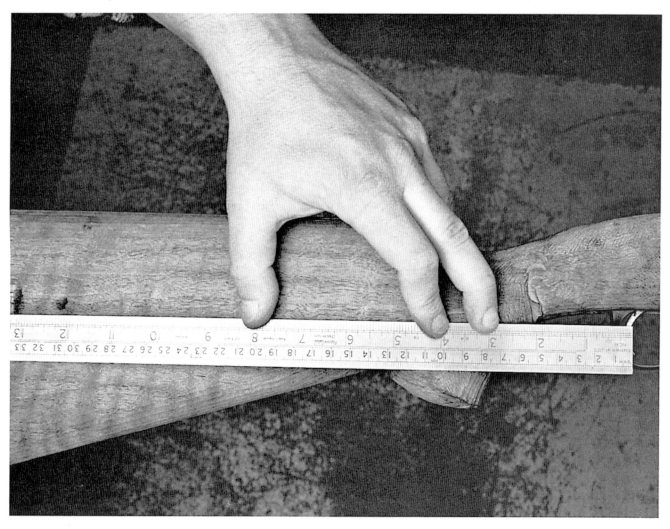

Figure 2-4

Figure 2-4 illustrates the method used to measure the length of pull on a stock. An approximation of this measurement, and only an approximation, can be made by grasping the stock by the pistol grip and noting the distance from the center of the trigger to the inside bend of the shooter's elbow, and then cut the stock a little longer than that measurement. Then proceed as outlined in the text.

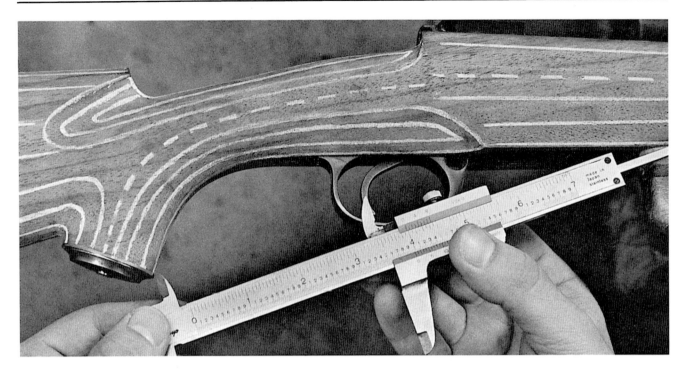

Figure 2-5

Locating the Leading Edge of the Grip-cap
Figures 2-5 and 2-6

The location of the leading edge of the grip-cap dictates the length and (in part) the front curvature of the grip, which are important to the overall handling qualities and pointability of the rifle. A rifle is most easily pointed when the forearm, wrist, and trigger finger are aligned in a straight line.

The length of the grip is determined by the length and width of the individual shooter's hand. The front curvature of the grip is determined by the way in which the shooter holds the rifle after it is mounted to his shoulder. In general, the shooter who holds his forearm more parallel to the ground in his shooting stance, will require less curvature on the front of the grip than the shooter whose forearm angles downward toward the ground and requires more curvature on the front of the grip to align the forearm, wrist, and trigger finger.

Two measurements are needed to locate the front edge of the grip-cap. Figure 2-5 illustrates the diagonal measurement from the center of the trigger to the leading edge of the grip-cap. On a modern bolt action sporter stock this measurement will generally be between 3-1/4" and 4-1/2".

Finish Shaping the Stock

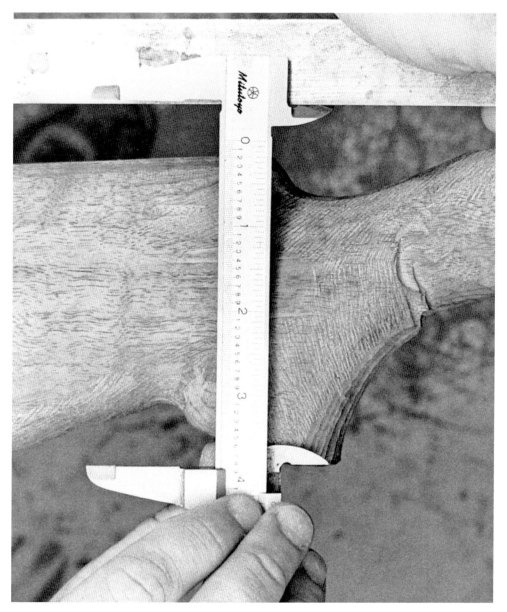

Figure 2-6

Figure 2-6 illustrates the measurement of the perpendicular distance from the center of the trigger to the leading edge of the grip-cap. Depending on the width of the shooter's hand, this measurement will generally be between 1-3/8" to 1-5/8".

The easiest way to make this measurement is to lay a straightedge along the top of the stock and measure first to the center of the trigger, add the desired distance and use that measurement to locate the depth of the leading edge of the grip.

Drop at the Heel and Comb
Figures 2-7 and 2-8

The comb of the stock supports the shooter's head, placing his eye at the correct height, and directly in line with the sights.

With the sights in place, the comb is gradually cut down and the cheekpiece changed as necessary until the eye is aligned with the plane of the sights. Then remove an additional 1/16" from the comb, for most shooters mount a gun with the head held higher when the mounting is deliberate, as in a shop fitting situation. (Note that pitch can make a difference in the comb height and should be determined prior lowering the comb.)

To determine initial dimensions of the comb, start with the nose of the comb just low enough to clear the cocking piece of the bolt. On a scope-sighted rifle make the initial drop at the heel the same as the drop at the nose of the comb, and adjust from there. If the rifle is to be used with iron sights use the same starting height at the nose of the comb, and cut the heel 1/2" lower, then adjust.

Generally the drop at the nose of the comb will vary only slightly from the starting dimension. Drop at the heel may vary up to an inch, or more.

The comb is planed down with a 9-1/2" plane and checked for flatness with a piece of ground die stock as shown in Figures 2-7 and 2-8.

Finish Shaping the Stock

Figure 2-7

Figure 2-8

Cast-off

Figure 2-9

For a right-handed shooter, cast-off is the distance the buttstock bends to the right of center, and cast-on is the distance to the left of center. For a left-handed shooter measurements are reversed. The function of cast is to position the shooter's eye in line with the barrel and sights. A rifle with cast-off is slightly quicker in target acquisition. However, cast-off makes a rifle pivot slightly inward as it recoils and should only be used on light or moderate recoiling rifles. Either a straight stock or a stock with a small amount of cast-on should be used on heavy recoiling rifles. Cast-on causes a slight outward movement (away from the shooter's face) of the buttstock during recoil.

Cast-off and toe-out, Figure 2-11, traditionally originate at the rear guard screw, flow through the pistol-grip and terminate at the geometric center of the buttplate. This, however, results in a pistol-grip that is out of line with the vertical axis of the stock which impairs the handling qualities and pointability of the rifle. The author prefers to carry a straight line though the pistol-grip and start the cast at the nose of the comb and the toe-out starts at the rear of the grip-cap. This complicates the shaping of the rear of the grip but the resulting improvement in handling qualities gained through using an "in line" grip are more than worth the extra time shaping.

To establish the top center line of the buttstock, a thin nylon string is threaded through the barrel. Pull this string tight and center it on the rear guardscrew hole and the cocking piece raceway in the tang. See Figure 2-9. Transfer this line in pencil to the top of the buttstock. The cast-off and cast-on dimensions are measured from this line.

Finish Shaping the Stock

Figure 2-9

Figure 2-9 illustrates a method used to establish the top center line of the buttstock and wrist.

Pitch and Toe-Out

Figures 2-10 and 2-11

Pitch is the angle across the heel and toe of the stock relative to the boreline. Toe is the distance from the vertical center of the boreline to the toe of the stock. For a right-handed shooter "toe-out" would be the distance of the toe to the right of the vertical center of the boreline.

The combined function of pitch and toe-out is to maximize the contact between the butt and the shooter's shoulder. By maximizing this contact the chance of the butt slipping during recoil is minimized and the felt recoil is diminished because the recoil is distributed over a greater area.

To demonstrate the need for pitch and toe-out, place a straightedge into the pocket formed on the shoulder where the butt is mounted. The straightedge will slope outward and downward, away from the shooter's face. From this we see that for a buttplate to fit the shoulder properly the heel of the stock must be longer than the toe (pitch) and, for a right-handed shooter, the toe of the stock must be offset to the right (toe-out).

In general, the more heavily built through the shoulders and chest, the more down-pitch and toe-out that shooter will require.

However, too much down-pitch is undesirable as it will cause the butt of the stock to snag in the shooter's clothing and be slow to mount. It may also cause the barrel to point low if the rifle is mounted quickly. It is this angling of the barrel, combined with the force vectors involved in recoil, that makes a gun with too much down-pitch slide upward during recoil. (Conversely, a gun with too little down-pitch will slide down the shoulder when fired and when mounted quickly will point too high.) In addition there is a direct relationship between the amount of pitch and the amount of drop at the heel of the stock. In order to compensate for the downward rotation of the rifle at the muzzle, stocks with too much down-pitch often have too much drop at the heel. Too much drop at the heel increases the rotational force vector of recoil, and when combined with the stock slippage due to too much down-pitch, makes a rifle so stocked sin-

Finish Shaping the Stock

Figure 2-10

In Figure 2-10 a paper template is used to layout the pitch on a buttstock. The center of the template is centered on the desired length of pull mark. The pitch is set by rotating the template until the toe is the correct distance "shorter" than the heel of the stock.

gularly unpleasant and painful to shoot *in any caliber.*

Probably the best method for determining the amount of pitch an individual needs is to loosen the buttplate of an existing stock and insert shims under the toe and heel until the barrel of the rifle is parallel with the ground when the shooter mounts the gun naturally. The shooter should have his eyes closed when this test is made to avoid the natural tendency to correct barrel position. A helper will be needed to judge when the barrel is in the correct plane. The objective is to make the correct mounting the rifle completely automatic, requiring no conscious effort or adjustment once the rifle is shouldered.

PROFESSIONAL STOCKMAKING

Figure 2-11

In Figure 2-11 the top center of the buttplate is aligned with the desired cast-off measurement and the toe of the buttplate is moved to the right to get the toe-out dimension. This stock had 1/4" cast-off and 3/8" toe-out.

Finish Shaping the Stock

Once the correct pitch has been determined, lay one leg of a framing square along the top of the stock with the other leg touching the heel at the butt of the stock. Measure the distance between the toe of the stock and the leg of the square to determine how much shorter than the heel the toe of the stock must be in order to get the correct down-pitch. Transfer these measurements to the new stock by simply making the toe that much less than the heel when the center of the buttplate or pad is at the desired length of pull. Any stock, measured from the bore line and laid out as described above will have the correct pitch for that particular shooter regardless of the length of pull or the length of the barrel of the rifle.

Shaping the Stock

Section 2
Introduction to the tools used in shaping
Figures 2-12 through 2-32

A short discussion of the tools used during the shaping process is in order. Often several different tools, or combinations of tools, can be used for shaping the same area of the stock. At other times only one tool will best shape that particular area.

In choosing which tool, or tools, to use the stockmaker should consider several factors. The first is quite simply which tool(s) will do the job. For example, if there is a large amount of excess wood to be removed such as during the initial bevel shaping of the buttstock, the stockmaker may choose to remove the bulk of the wood with the rasp or spokeshave and then smooth and define the bevel with a nine-inch smoothing plane, or the stockmaker may decide to use the rasp or the plane exclusively to do the job. On the other hand, during the finish shaping of the stock where very little wood is being removed and the use of a rasp might leave compression marks under the surface of the wood, the stockmaker may decide to use either a plane or a smooth cut file to bring the wood down to its final dimensions. Both or either tool will get the job done. This leads us to the second factor that the stockmaker must consider, personal preference. Every stockmaker has certain tools that he likes to use, more importantly, that he feels comfortable and confident in using. These tools almost become extensions of the stockmaker's hands and eyes and automatically seem to do what the stockmaker wants them to do with little thought or guidance. The author has several such tools that are constantly on his bench, and although they may often not be the best or most efficient tools for doing a particular job, they are the tools that are most frequently reached for.

Not everyone will be able to master each and every tool used in stockmaking. In fact, two people using the very same tool will often wind up with very different results. I once watched an English-trained stockmaker completely shape the buttstock of a side-lock shotgun using nothing more than a draw knife and a smooth-cut rasp. The results were amazing and the stock was completely shaped in a matter of hours. Several days later, however, I watched an American colleague of mine try to duplicate the feat of the Englishman, only to have the drawknife bite too deep in several places, completely and irretrievably ruining a stock that he had spent many hours inletting. If you ask the Englishman what tool works best to shape a stock he would answer the drawknife. I can't print my American colleague views on this tool however. Alvin Linden, the eccentric Swedish genius of a stockmaker, often used a hewing ax for the gross removal of wood from his stocks, but only if the stock had correct "chopping grain." Would I recommend either of these tools? Not on your life. I've tried the drawknife and it scared the hell out of me. Yet John Bivins regularly uses a short German drawknife to rough shape the buttstocks of his exquisite longrifles. As for Alvin Linden's hewing ax, I'll leave that for you to try. What it boils down to is that you should use whatever tool that works best for you and will get the job done.

The Smooth-cut Plane

Figures 2-12 through 2-15

Due to its ability to cut flat and level lines this plane is used throughout the shaping of the stock. In fact, most of the shaping of the top and right side of the buttstock, the sides (or body) of the stock, and the bottom and sides of the forearm are shaped with the 9-1/2" smooth plane. The plane removes wood in a very controlled manner and can be adjusted to either remove large amounts of wood at a time, making it useful for rough shaping the stock, or it can be adjusted to remove the paper thin shavings desirable during the finish shaping procedures. Because planes, like chisels, remove wood through a cutting action (leaving a smooth surface to the wood), they can be used to shape the stock down to its final dimensions without fear of damaging or bruising the wood beneath the surface.

In order for the plane to cut properly the blade of the plane must be sharpened at the proper angle. (Many plane blades have the proper sharpening angle engraved on the blade.) In addition, three adjustments must be made to adjust the plane for cutting wood the hardness of that found in gunstocks. The first adjustment is setting the distance between the front of the blade and the body of the plane. This distance is called the "throat" of the plane and for hardwoods the throat should be set to approximately 1/8". To set the throat of the plane first remove the lever-cap (hopefully self-explanatory) and then the blade assembly from the plane. You will note that the blade assembly sits on a slanted platform which is called the "frog" of the plane. On top of the frog there are two screws. Loosen these two screws slightly and replace the blade assembly and lever-cap onto the plane. Now, on the back of the frog you will find the adjustment screw that moves the frog forward and backward. Turn this screw to adjust the throat to approximately 1/8-inch wide. Then remove the lever cap and blade assembly and tighten the two screws on top to the frog. The second adjustment to the plane is done on the blade assembly. First remove the assembly from the plane. The blade assembly consists of two parts, the blade proper (which is called the iron) and the chip-braker or cap-iron that fits on the side of the blade opposite the sharpening bevel. To cut hardwood efficiently, the leading edge of the chip-breaker should be positioned within 1/32-inch of the front edge of the blade. Loosen the blade assembly screw and adjust the cap-iron (chip-breaker) accordingly. The third adjustment sets the plane's depth of cut the amount that the blade projects below the bottom of the plane and is controlled by the large adjustment wheel located between the rear grip and the back of the frog. To adjust the depth, first turn the plane upside down and sight down the bottom (sole) of the plane. If the edge of the blade projects above the bottom, turn the adjustment wheel until the edge of the blade disappears below the surface. Then, while still sighting along the bottom of the plane, reverse the direction of the adjustment wheel, pushing the blade outward until just a thin sliver (0.007-0.010″) of the blade projects above the sole of the plane. Only experience and the cuttability of the individual piece of wood will dictate the optimal depth setting of the blade.

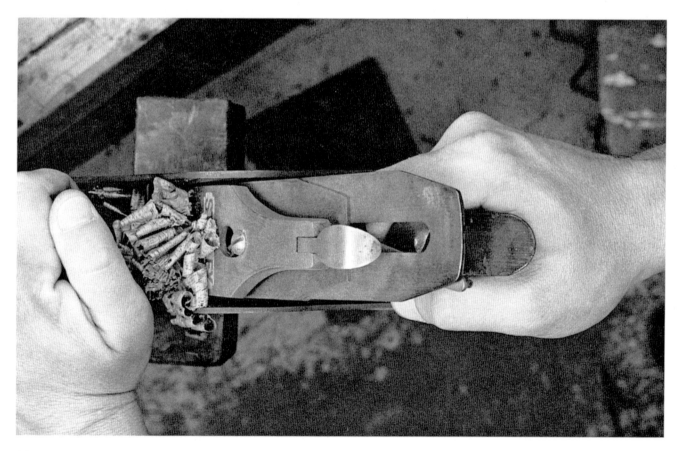

Figure 2-12

Figure 2-13

Figures 2-13 and 2-14 illustrate the hand positions used for long straight forward cuts with the plane. (Examples of these cuts would be the top of the comb, the sides of the body of the stock through the receiver area, and the sides and bottom of the forearm.) In use, the plane is held with the wrists in a semi-locked position and pushed forward along the prevailing line flow of that area of the stock. The stock should be positioned in the vise so that the desired finished plane (axis) of the cut is parallel to the floor and at or slightly below the height of the stockmaker's right elbow. Positioning the stock in this manner gives the stockmaker better control of the tool in that his right forearm and hand move parallel to the floor while simultaneously moving parallel to the axis of the finished cut. This not only provides the best leverage for the cut, allowing the stockmaker to lean forward slightly and put the weight of his body into the force necessary to push the plane forward, but also allows the stockmaker to control the angle of the cut simply by keeping his right forearm parallel to the floor which is in turn parallel to the plane of the desired cut.

Finish Shaping the Stock

Figure 2-14

Figure 2-14 illustrates the 24-inch jointer plane. Because of its 24-inch sole this plane is capable of planing surfaces smooth and level to within several thousandths of an inch. When stocking from a square blank this plane is used to smooth and level the blank. With the semi-inletted stock its use is mainly confined to planing the profile lines of the body and forearm of the stock.

Figure 2-15 illustrates another method of using the 9-1/2-inch plane. In this technique the plane is angled slightly and then pushed sideways along the prevailing flow lines of the stock. Angling the plane like this presents a narrower section of blade to the wood, thus producing a narrower and more highly controlled cut. Note the width of the curls in Figure 2-15 versus those in Figures 2-13 and 2-14.

In addition, angling the plane places the edge of the blade closer to the leading edge of the tool which allows the stockmaker to use this tool in those areas behind the grip and at the sides of the front of the comb where the more conventional "straight-on use" would be precluded by the overhang of the nose of the plane in front of the blade. When using this technique the tool is guided by the stockmaker's hands and forearms which move parallel to the axis (plane) of the desired cut. All of the cutting force for the cut comes from the arms pushing straight away from the stockmaker's body along the direction of the flow lines of the stock.

This technique, used in conjuncture with a coarse blade setting, is useful for hogging off large controlled amounts of wood during the rough shaping of the stock. When used with a fine blade setting this technique is used extensively during the final shaping where the narrow cuts are used to gradually round over the curves of the stock.

Finish Shaping the Stock

Figure 2-15

Figure 2-15 illustrates the 9-1/2-inch plane shaping one of the initial shaping bevels on a stock being shaped from the square blank.

Professional Stockmaking

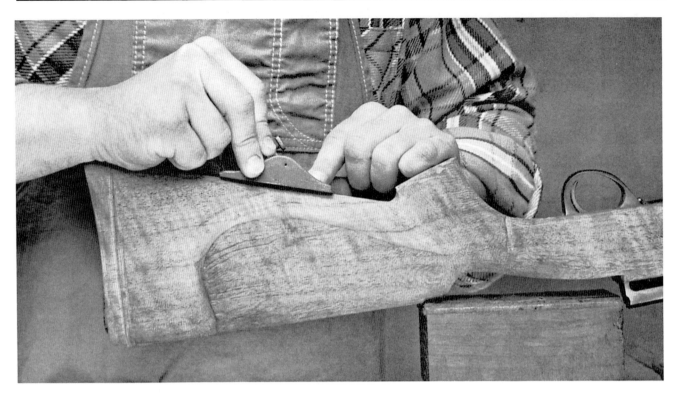

Figure 2-16

The Palm Plane

Figures 2-16 and 2-17

Figures 2-16 and 2-17 illustrate the use of the palm plane during the final shaping of the stock. It is a handy tool to use for the final rounding over and leveling of the lower sides and toe-line of the buttstock and can also be used on the bottom and sides of the forearm. Palm planes generally lack the precise adjustments of the larger planes, and to adjust the depth of cut on this particular plane involves a trial and error method of tapping the top of the blade with a rawhide mallet until a satisfactory cutting action is obtained. The use of this tool does have its drawback however in that due to the short length of the plane it is possible to plane bumps or dips into areas that should be flat. Therefore, in order to maintain a flat and level surface the stockmaker must frequently check the lines of the work both visually and with a proven straightedge. (Authors note: if anyone ever sees, knows of or has the urge to make a plane this size that is fully adjustable, please let me know. I will be first in line to buy one.)

Finish Shaping the Stock

Figure 2-17

Figure 2-17 illustrates the palm plane being used during the finish shaping and rounding of the forearm of the stock.

The Bull Nose Plane

Figures 2-18 and 2-19

In Figures 2-18 and 2-19 the nose of a palm plane has been cut off to make it a Bull Nose or chisel plane. This is the most specialized plane on my bench and is only used to straighten the last 1/4" - 3/8" between the toe-line and the sides and bottom of the rear of the pistol-grip, and also at the back of the ghost line of the cheekpiece. Due to its short length this plane must be used with extreme care and only with light cuts, as it constantly wants to dig in and nose dive into the wood. Bull Nose planes (with removable noses) and chisel planes with longer bases are commercially available and may be a better tool to use. However, since this plane has limited use, and over the years I have become accustomed to using it, I will probably keep it. If I were to replace it however it would be with a Stanley #92 Rabbet plane whose removable top converts it into a chisel plane.

Finish Shaping the Stock

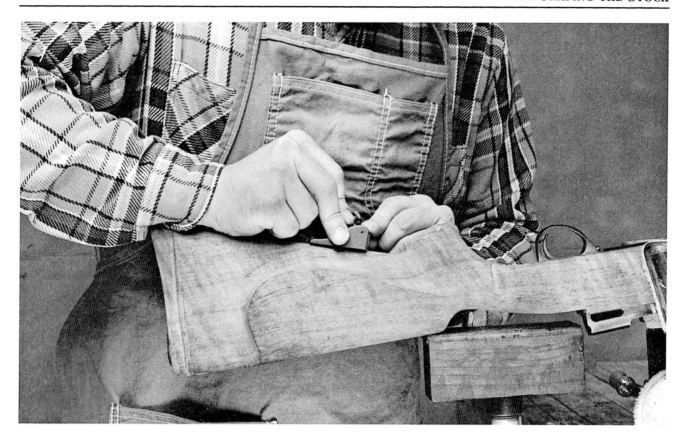

Figure 2-18

Figure 2-19

The Spokeshave

Figure 2-20

Figure 2-20 illustrates the use of the spokeshave in rough shaping the initial bevel under the cheekpiece. With the exception of the drawknife, no other tool commonly found on the stockmaker's bench will remove wood faster or more efficiently than the spokeshave. The tool does have its drawbacks in that it has a very short base which makes it difficult to form perfectly straight and level surfaces over longer distances. For roughing out the initial bevel cuts during the rough shaping of the buttstock and forearm, however, this tool is hard to beat. This tool should be used only for roughing out these bevels. The final smoothing and leveling of the bevels should be done with either a smooth-cut pattern maker's rasp or the 9-1/2" smoothing plane.

Although I have never tried one, the Kunz firm also makes a half-round spokeshave with a concave face and blade which just may be the ticket for roughing out the curves of the pistol-grip and the top of the wrist. It may also work well on the underside of the forearm, although, once again, due to its short base I would be leery about using it to shape the longer areas.

The spokeshave works best when used to cut with the grain in fairly straight grain wood. In gnarly or brash wood, or when used to cut against the grain, the short base of the spokeshave allows it to tip into the wood leaving an uneven surface or tearing out chunks of wood. (The degree of unevenness or tearing will vary according to the cuttability of the individual blank and the heaviness or depth of the cut being taken.) The tool can either be pushed or pulled through the wood. Once again, the stockmaker's hand and arms should move parallel to the desired plane or axis of the finish cut.

Finish Shaping the Stock

Figure 2-20

The spokeshave is a fun tool to use, and although the work must be frequently checked for flatness with the straightedge, in the hands of an experienced stockmaker most of the rough shaping of the stock can be accomplished with this tool alone. For the author, this tool evokes the greatest sense of actually sculpting the square blank into a stock. The author also freely admits that he has gotten carried away and come damn close to ruining a stock or two through the exuberant overuse of this tool however, so be careful!

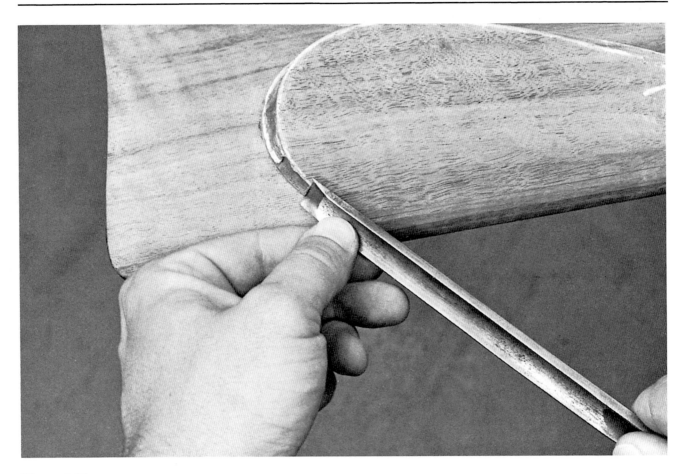

Figure 2-21

The In-cannel Gouge
Figures 2-21 through 2-23

Although limited to specific areas of use, gouges are capable of removing large amounts of wood in a very controlled manner and leave a clean surface to the wood, and are therefore used during both the rough and the finish shaping of the stock. Figure 2-21 illustrates this gouge completing the final detailing of the cove on the cheekpiece. Figures 2-22 and 2-23 illustrate the use of the in-cannel gouge in rough shaping the comb fluting.

By now, having used this chisel extensively during the inletting of the barreled action and also for the rough removal of excess wood during the profiling of the stock, this tool should be an old friend to the stockmaker. However, I repeat for the umpteenth time this chisel must be razor sharp and that a push-pull muscle control is necessary to control the depth, cut, and forward motion of the tool.

FINISH SHAPING THE STOCK

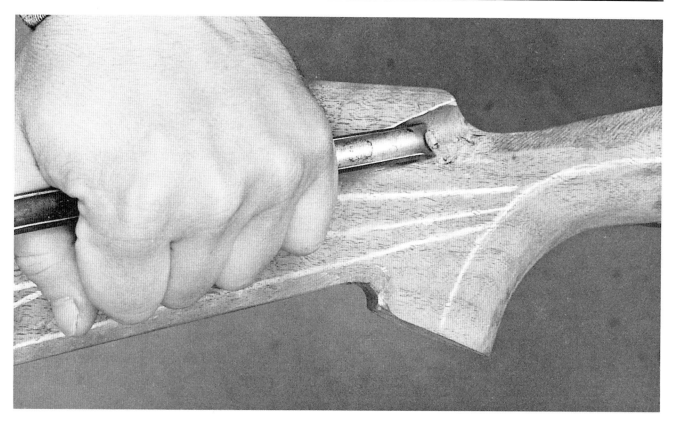

Figure 2-22

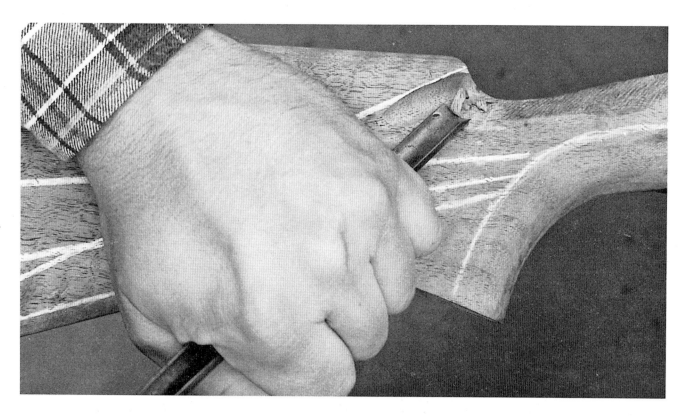

Figure 2-23

113

The Straight Chisels
Figures 2-24 through 2-26

Figures 2-24 through 2-26 illustrate the straight chisels used in shaping the stock. Like the gouges, the straight chisels are generally limited to specific tasks or jobs during the shaping. They are however, the tools that I find best suited to shape those specific areas of the stock.

In Figure 2-24 the modified deep-mortice chisel is being used to remove and level the excess wood below the rear of the cheekpiece during the rough shaping of the buttstock.

The long side of the chisel, which acts much the same as the sole of the plane in guiding and leveling the cut, is placed flat against the previously shaped portion of the stock. The chisel is then advanced forward in a series of narrow light cuts along the flow lines of the stock. This procedure is repeated until all of the excess wood has been removed and that portion of the stock is shaped in a continuum of the shape of the stock directly behind it. When used "long-side down" the modified deep-mortice chisel is probably the best tool for the gross removal of the excess wood from directly beneath the cheekpiece during the rough shaping of the buttstock.

Finish Shaping the Stock

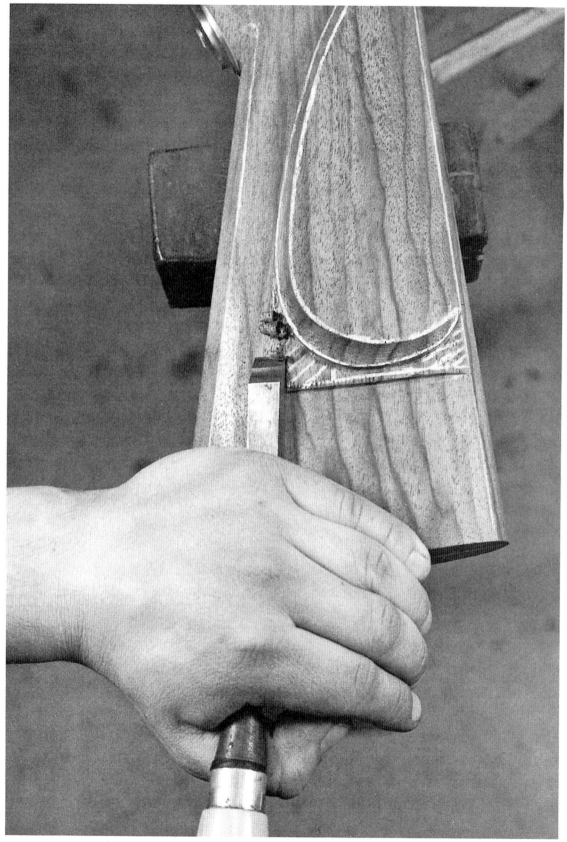

Figure 2-24

Figure 2-25

In Figure 2-25 the deep-mortice chisel is used to outline the edge of the ghostline of the cheekpiece. A light downward pressure is exerted by the right hand while the left hand and thumb position, push, and guide the blade of the chisel around the edge of the ghostline. Note that the chisel is at a slight angle from true vertical so that only the rear portion of the chisel's blade is used to make the actual cut. (Although a narrower chisel could have been used here, this chisel is one of the author's favorite tools and the size and weight of this tool acutally helps to control the cut. The reader may, however, wish to use a narrower chisel, a number 2 or number 3 gouge, or even a fishtail chisel to make this particular cut.)

Finish Shaping the Stock

Figure 2-26

After the ghostline of the cheekpiece has been outlined, as in Figure 2-25, the excess wood immediately behind the upper part of the cheekpiece can be removed with the 1-1/4" paring chisel as shown in Figure 2-26. Unlike the deep-mortice chisel which was designed to cut in a straight downward or forward motion, the paring chisel's thin blade was designed to shear the wood in a sideways sliding or "paring" motion. The side of the chisel is aligned with the flow line of the stock, and while the right hand exerts a small amount of forward pressure, the left hand guides and pushes the tool to the right shearing of a small curl of wood from behind the cheekpiece.

The Nicholson 50 Rasp

Figures 2-27 through 2-29

Mastering the technique of rasping a perfectly flat and straight line is extremely important if the stockmaker is to have total control over the shape of the stock. Although planes are used to establish and shape the majority of the straight lines of the stock, there are places that the plane simply can't reach or where the rasp is handier to use. At times you will find yourself reaching for the rasp, even though a plane could be used for the same job. It's simply a handy and efficient tool to use.

The Nicholson No. 50 patternmaker's rasp illustrated in Figures 2-27 through 2-29 is perhaps the finest and most versatile rasp available to the stockmaker. It is found on the bench of almost every serious stockmaker, and is the only rasp that this author can unconditionally recommend for use in shaping stocks.

Unlike most other rasps, the shallow staggered-tooth design of the Nicholson 50 produces a remarkably clean and smooth surface with very shallow tooth marks and little or no damage to the wood beneath the surface. It can therefore be used for shaping the stock down to almost finish dimensions. Any compression marks left below the surface of the wood by this rasp will be minor and are re-expanded and raised to the surface of the stock with steam during the sanding operations.

When rasping over longer distances, it is extremely important that you use a proven straightedge to frequently check the surface of the rasp cut for any dips or bumps that must be corrected. This is especially important during the final shaping of the stock where the correction of a 1/16" dip in a line could entail changing the entire shape of an area. Two hints: 1) coating the edge of the straightedge with inletting black and then placing it on the surface being rasped or planed will quickly reveal any high or low spots that need attention; 2) mark any low spots with a brightly colored wax pencil as a reminder not to remove any further wood from that spot, and then work outward from each end of the low spot until the entire surface is smooth and level.

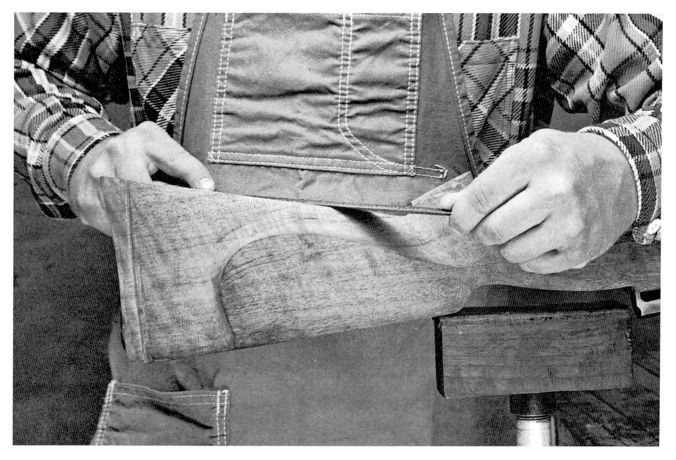

Figure 2-27

The Nicholson 50 rasp is also used to smooth and level wood in areas that other tools can't effectively reach. In Figure 2-17 the toe-line of the stock had to be moved up slightly in order to adjust to a small change made in the curvature of the grip during the final shaping operations. Although a palm plane was used to level the wood from the toe of the stock to within approximately 2-1/2 to 3 inches behind the pistol-grip, it was ineffective from this point forward due to the nose of the plane running into the back of the grip. Although the modified palm plane (chisel plane) was considered for the planing these last couple of inches, its use was rejected due to the questionable ability of its short base to plane a level surface 3 inches long, therefore the rasp was chosen for the job.

In Figure 2-27 note that the rasp is held both perpendicular to the geometric geometric center of the buttstock and also at a slight angle to the long axis of the line being rasped. The modified drawfiling technique described in Figures 2-28 and 2-29 is used to complete and level this cut.

In Figure 2-28 the flat side of the rasp is being used to shape the first shaping bevel on the lower right side of the buttstock. The following is a description of the best technique that the author has found for the controlled rasping of the long straight lies found on gunstocks. This technique is harder to describe in words than it is to actually do on the wood. A little practice and trial and error experimentation will convince you that it is an easy and effective technique for the controlled rasping of long straight lines however. For lack of a better name, and because this technique involves elements of drawfiling, the technique will be referred to as "modified drawfiling."

Hold the rasp at a slight angle to the long axis of the line to be cut. Then, while simultaneously pushing the rasp forward (along its long axis) slide the rasp sideways along the line or plane of the desired cut. (i.e., the rasp is moved forward and sideways at the same time). The rasp is held with both hands with the wrist in a semi-locked position with the forearms. The cut is controlled by moving both your hands and forearms parallel to the plane of the desired finish cut. As long as your hands and forearms move the face of the rasp in a perfectly straight line, the tool will cut a flat surface.

The ratio of how fast you push the rasp forward versus sideways depends on the amount of wood to be removed. The more wood that needs to be removed, the more you push the rasp forward as opposed to sideways. Conversely, the less wood that needs to be removed, the more you slide the rasp sideways and the less you push it forward. Experience and the amount of wood to be removed will quickly tell you how much of each movement to use.

Often the section of wood that must be removed will be thicker at one end to the line flow than the other. In general, but with exceptions, it is better to start rasping at the thicker end. Establish the direction of the cut, and the plane of the cut, parallel to the plane of the desired finish cut. Then gradually lengthen the surface of the cut until it extends the entire length of the desired line.

Finish Shaping the Stock

Figure 2-28

The curved side of the Nicholson 50 rasp is used in the modified drawfiling motion to rough shape the front and sides of the pistol-grip and finger clearance arch. Note that only the trailing edge of the rasp, i.e., that portion of the rasp from the center of the curvature to the rear edge, is used to remove and shape the wood during the modified drawfiling movements described here.

As when using the flat side of the rasp, the ratio of the curved side moving straight ahead versus sliding sideways is determined by the amount of wood that needs to be removed. During the rough shaping or beveling of the sides of the grip, as in Figure 2-29, where a lot of wood has to be removed quickly, the rasp is advanced forward and pushed sideways at approximately the same rate. However, when used to blend two curved areas where little wood needs to be removed, the rasp is advanced forward very little, with most of its movement directed sideways along the plane(s) of the desired contour of the cut.

Once again, only experimentation and experience will tell you how much and in which direction to move the rasp. A word of caution concerning the use of the rasp in shaping the wrist and pistol-grip of the stock. Due to the quick cutting ability of the Nicholson 50 it is easy to get into trouble very quickly when using this rasp in these areas. Unlike the buttstock and forearm whose gently curved contours can easily be seen and rasped with the flat side of the Nicholson 50, the tight curves and tapered contours of the pistol-grip, wrist, and finger clearance arch must be developed and shaped slowly if mistakes are to be avoided. For that reason the author strongly suggests that the Nicholson 50 rasp should only be used to rough shape these areas, and then only if used very carefully. The final development of the line flows and contours in these areas should be done with a tool called the crossing file which will be discussed next. A word to the wise, or a slab-sided wrist and grip to the unwise, should be sufficient.

Finish Shaping the Stock

Figure 2-29

The Crossing File

Figures 2-30 through 2-32

Figures 2-30 through 2-32 illustrate several of the many uses of the 8-inch "0" cut crossing file. This is the best tool the author has found for the final shaping and blending of the curved line flows and radii of the wrist, pistol-grip, and finger clearance arch of the stock. In the "0" cut pattern this tool removes wood quickly and yet in a very controllable manner.

Crossing files have two curved sides, each having a different radius. One side has the same radius as the standard 8-inch half round file, while the other side has a larger radius of flatter curvature. These files taper to a point in both width and thickness and are generally double-cut on both sides.

It is the tapered shape and dual radii of this file that makes it so useful to the stockmaker. Instead of having to use a different file to shape each separate contour or radius of the stock, the stockmaker simply uses that portion of the crossing file which most closely matches the shape or radius of the desired cut.

In Figure 2-30, the tip of the crossing file is being used in a modified drawfiling movement to shape and blend the lower rear sides of the pistol-grip. All of the cutting force for this cut comes from an upward flipping (or rotation) of the wrists which gradually wears away the wood to shape and blend the short, complex radii and contours of this area. The radii on both sides of the file are used to shape this area of the stock.

Hint: During the final shaping of the stock, think of the wood as a piece of clay that you are pushing and molding with the files. Gradually walk the file along each flow line and contour of the stock, watching not only the path of the cut on the surface of the wood, but also the line of cutting debris or dust that the file leaves in its wake. Watching both the cut and the dust gives a better indication of the true direction of each cut than can be gained by watching either individually. (Note the direction of the filing dust in Figures 2-31 and 2-32.)

This section on the use of the crossing file completes the introduction to the tools the author uses in shaping the stock. It must be noted

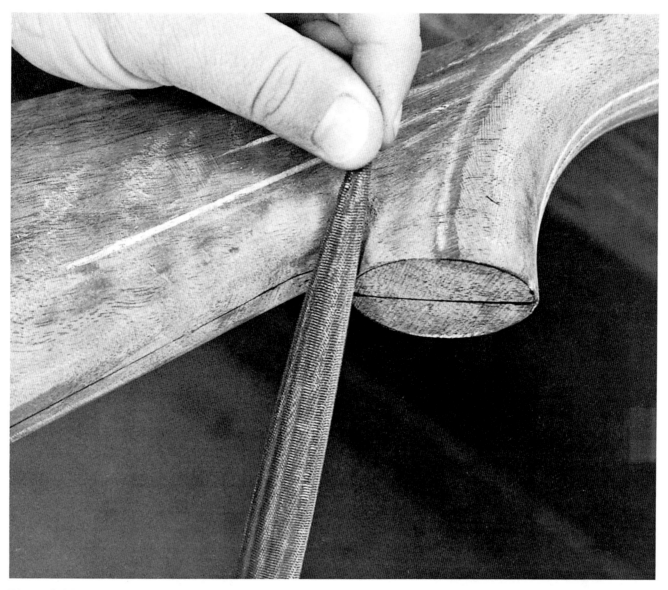

Figure 2-30

that these are not the only tools used for shaping however, and other tools will be introduced at their appropriate places throughout the text on shaping. In addition, the reader is encouraged to try to experiment with other tools that fulfill the basic functions of the tools described here. For example, in place of the 9-1/2-inch smooth plane or the Nicholson 50 rasp, the reader may want to try using one of the excellent Stanley Surform tools. The author can only suggest what tools and techniques work best for him. It is up to the individual reader to experiment with the different types of tools in order to determine which tool works best for him.

The crossing file can be used with either the modified drawfiling move-

Figure 2-31

ment as shown in Figure 2-30 or with a regular drawfiling movement in which the tool is only pushed sideways as shown in Figures 2-31 and 2-32. The stockmaker's hands and arms position and push the file along the plane

Finish Shaping the Stock

Figure 2-32

of the desired cut, using only the rear portion of the blade, from the center of the blade to the trailing edge, to make the actual cut.

Shaping the Stock

Section 3
Shaping Begins - Profiling the Buttstock
Figure 2-33

Once the length of pull, drop at the heel and comb, pitch, vertical depth of the buttplate or recoil pad, and the exact location of the leading edge of the grip-cap have been established, we are ready to profile the top and bottom lines of the buttstock. Figure 2-33 shows the completed profiles.

Line A is the comb-line of the buttstock. The dimensions of drop at the heel and comb were discussed in Figures 2-7 and 2-8.

Line B is the toe-line of the buttstock. It originates at the toe of the buttstock, flows upward through the pistol-grip, and terminates at a point even with or slightly above the rear guard screw, never below the screw. Stocks made with line B falling below the rear guard screw look, in Alvin Linden's words, "like a canoe paddle."

Line C, the curvature at the front of the pistol-grip, was discussed in Figure 2-5. This line originates at the leading edge of the grip-cap, and flows upward to intersect the extended toe-line of the stock at the rear guard screw. (A small change in line C will have a big effect on the way the stock feels and handles. Therefore line C should be left heavy at this stage to allow for final shaping after the sides and top of the wrist have been shaped down to near final dimensions.)

Finish Shaping the Stock

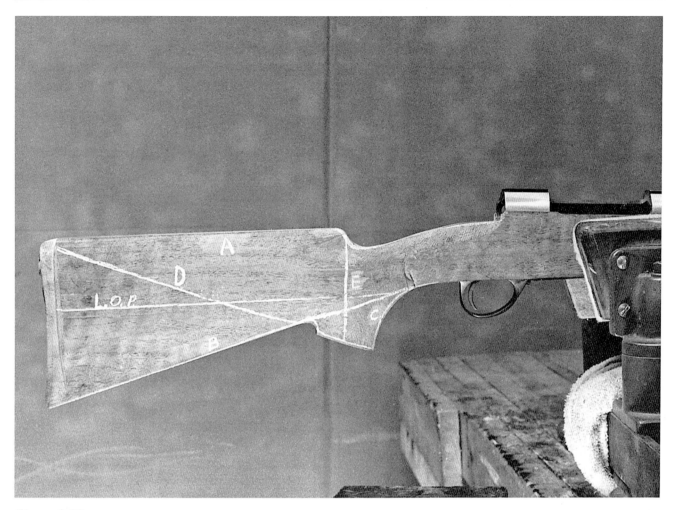

Figure 2-33

Line D determines the angle of the grip-cap. It originates at the leading edge of the grip, and depending on the stock's length of pull and personal tastes, extends to a point at or near the heel of the stock.

Line E, a perpendicular line dropped from the bore line of the rifle to the center of the grip-cap, is used to locate the nose of the comb. See Figures 2-37 and 2-38. Use a large carpenter's square laid along the top of the stock to locate and draw this line.

Rough Profiling the Toe-line of the Buttstock
Figures 2-34 through 2-36

Although not illustrated, the first step in rough profiling the lower buttstock is to rasp and file the bottom surface of the grip, line D Figure 2-33, perfectly flat and perpendicular to the vertical axis of the stock. The small notch behind the grip is then filed in with either a small chainsaw file or a fine cut rattail file.

The toe-line of the stock is then roughed in with the Nicholson #50 rasp as shown in Figure 2-34. The rasp is held at a slight angle to the work and used in the modified drawfiling motion as explained in Figures 2-27 through 2-29. The levelness of the cut is controlled by moving the rasp in the same plane as the desired cut.

The palm planes, Figure 2-35 and 2-36, are then used to smooth and remove any compression marks of the rasp from the toe-line.

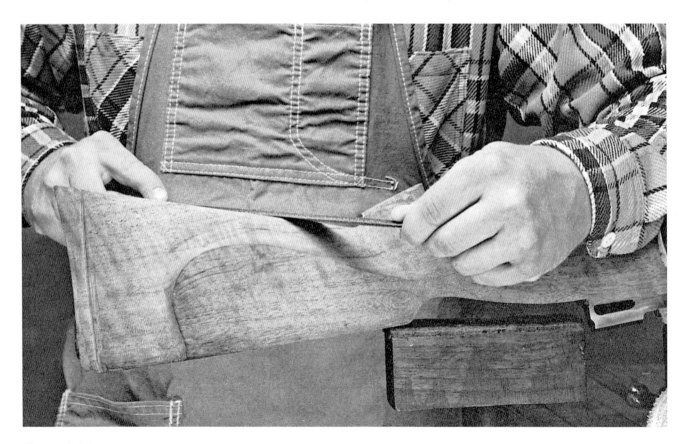

Figure 2-34

Finish Shaping the Stock

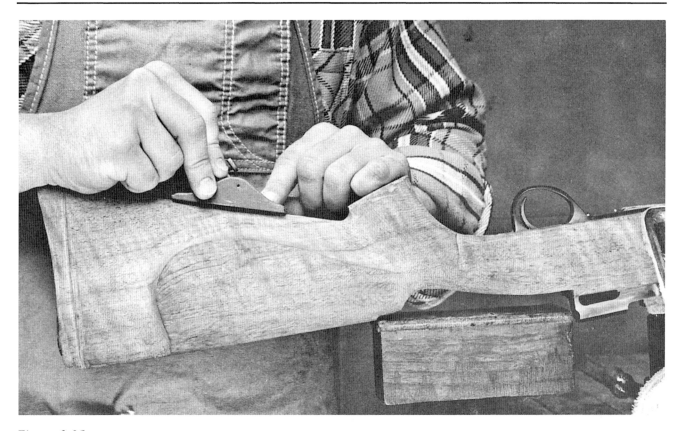

Figure 2-35

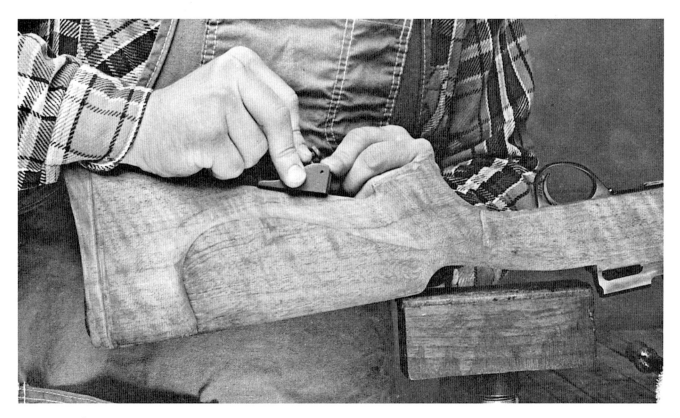

Figure 2-36

Profiling the Nose of the Comb
Figures 2-37 through 2-38

The nose of the comb will fall into an area from 1/4-inch in front of line E (see Figure 2-33) to perhaps 1/2- to 3/8-inch behind line E depending on the type of grip the shooter uses to hold the rifle. If the shooter uses a "Springfield thumb alongside the wrist" grip, the location of the nose of the comb is mainly cosmetic and it can be placed anywhere within the above parameters and still look good. If the shooter uses the "thumb across the top of the wrist hold" however, the nose of the comb must be cut back so as to not interfere with the shooter's thumb.

Try to make the lines of the nose of the comb and the radius between the nose of the comb and the top of the wrist as graceful as possible. In order to best judge how one profiling line blends into another, it often helps to step back from the bench and view the stock from a distance. Remove the wood slowly in the initial profiling, as the final shape and location of these points can only be determined during the final shaping and blending of the entire wrist and grip areas of the stock.

Finish Shaping the Stock

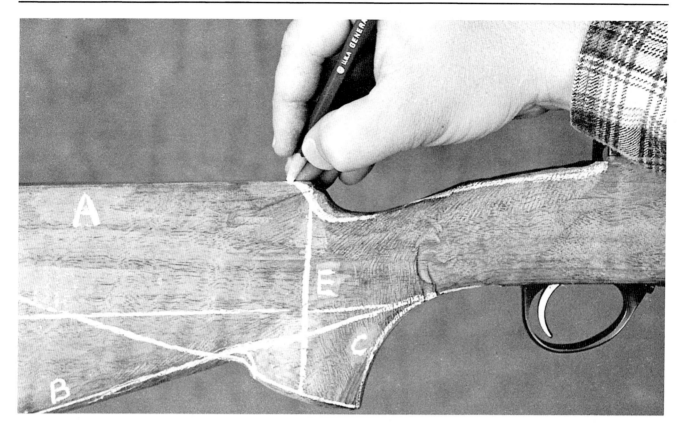

Figure 2-37

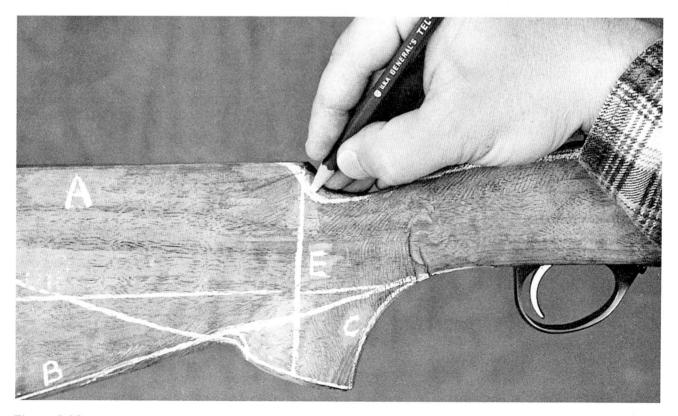

Figure 2-38

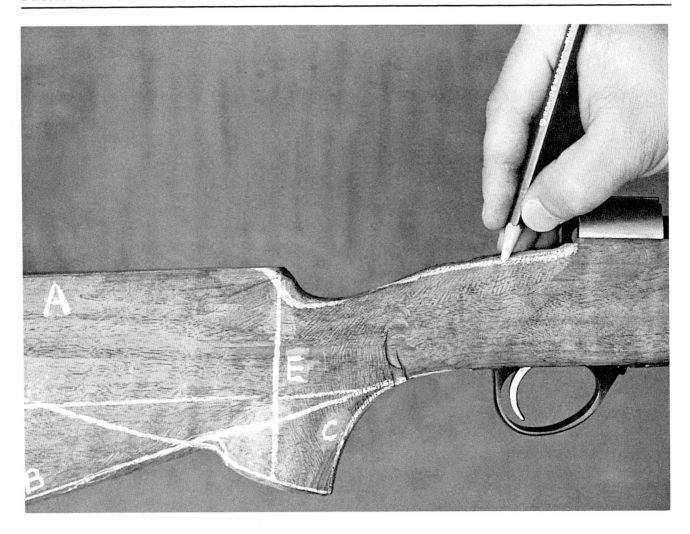

Figure 2-39

Layout of the Rough Profile Line on the Top of the Wrist
Figure 2-39

The profile of the top of the wrist flows upward and forward in a graceful line as shown in Figure 2-39. Note the thickness of the line being drawn. Since this is a rough layout line, extra wood should be left at this stage of the shaping to allow for small changes in this line as the shaping progresses. Also note that the fingers of the hand are braced against the top of the wrist as an aid in drawing this line.

Finish Shaping the Stock

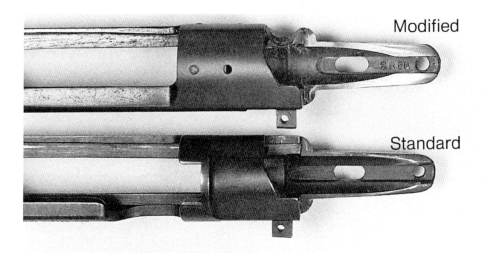

Figure 2-40

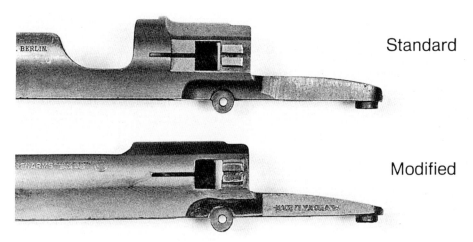

Figure 2-41

Modification of the Mauser Tang
Figures 2-40 and 2-41

In order to achieve a more pleasing line flow, and to avoid having to notch the wood directly behind the action's tang, the tang of both the Mauser and Sako actions should be modified as shown in Figures 2-40 and 2-41. Note that the top of the tang is filed right down to the bottom of the bolt raceway. Although the length of the tang on these actions is rather short, under 2 inches, their modified profile will determine the overall line flow on the top of the wrist. Therefore it is important that the modification shown be done correctly. A smooth cut file is the tool of choice. Work slowly, and carefully develop a pleasing line flow on the top of the tang.

Profiling the Sides of the Grip

Figure 2-42

Once the toe-line, comb and the bottom of the grip profiles have been established, the next step in shaping the buttstock is to profile the sides of the grip. The width of the grip is determined by the width of the grip-cap, which in turn is determined by the desired overall size and proportions of the completed rifle. The size and proportions of the completed rifle, in turn, are determined by the physical characteristics of the shooter, the rifle's caliber and expected recoil level, the desired weight of the rifle, and the strength of the individual stock blank or pre-turned stock. All of these factors must be taken into account when selecting the size and shape of the grip-cap to be used on a specific rifle. Lastly, the specific action being stocked, more appropriately perhaps, the shape of the tang of each action, alsoaffects the choice of the size of the grip-cap.

Mauser and Sako actions have a slender tang and thus in general can be stocked with slender grips and wrists. Model 70 Winchesters, Springfields, and Remington actions, however, have wide tangs that in general dictate a wider wrist and grip which require a wider grip-cap. One size does not fit all. A great deal of thought should go into the selection of the size and shape of the grip-cap for each specific rifle.

Position the grip-cap on the center line on the bottom of the grip and draw a heavy line around its circumference. Next, as a guide to rasping the grip the same thickness from front to back, measure the width of the grip-cap, divide by two, and mark out these half widths on both sides of the center line at the front and rear of the grip. Connect these points with a heavy line.

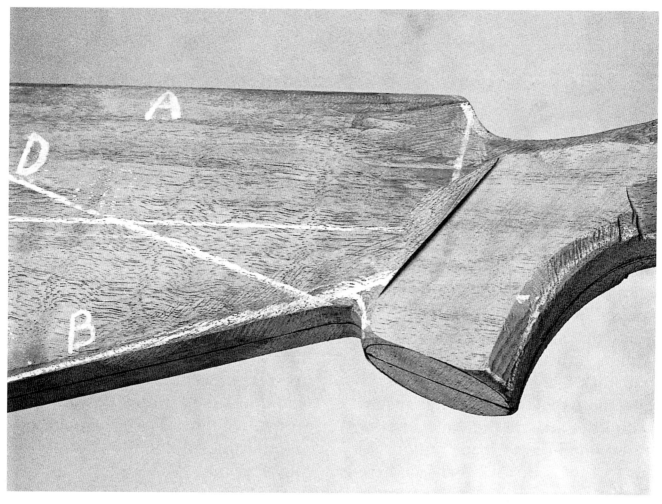

Figure 2-42

A Nicholson #50 and a wide fine cut file are then used to remove the wood outside of the lines denoting the grip-cap width as shown in Figure 2-42. Note that the rear boundary of this flat runs from the rear of the grip to a point just forward of the nose of the comb. Do not cut the rear boundary too far back. This flat should be cut straight across, from the bottom of the grip to the top of the wrist, with the width of the grip being equal at all points on the flat.

The flattening of the grip is an important benchmark used in shaping the stock. It not only lays out the initial width of the grip and wrist, but also lays out the width and taper of the buttstock directly behind the grip. Take your time and do it right initially and the subsequent shaping of these areas will be much easier.

Line Flow Diagram of the Buttstock
Section 4
Shaping the sides of the buttstock
Figure 2-43

Figure 2-43 illustrates the flow lines of the buttstock. A ruler placed along any of these straight lines should reveal a flat straight surface free of any bumps or dips. Study this illustration carefully. Although the left side of the buttstock has a cheekpiece that interrupts the line flow on that side, both sides are still the same and the entire line flow or shape of both sides of the buttstock is shown here. Line A slopes slightly upward from just below the heel to a point just below the nose of the comb.

Line B is almost parallel to the comb-line. Line C slopes slightly downward toward the wrist. Line D is the side profiling line of the buttstock and runs from the center of the butt to the center of the grip. Line E slopes upward to blend into the rear transition of the buttstock and grip. Line F slopes upward from just above the toe of the stock to the transitional line flow at the rear of the grip.

Also see Figure 2-55.

Finish Shaping the Stock

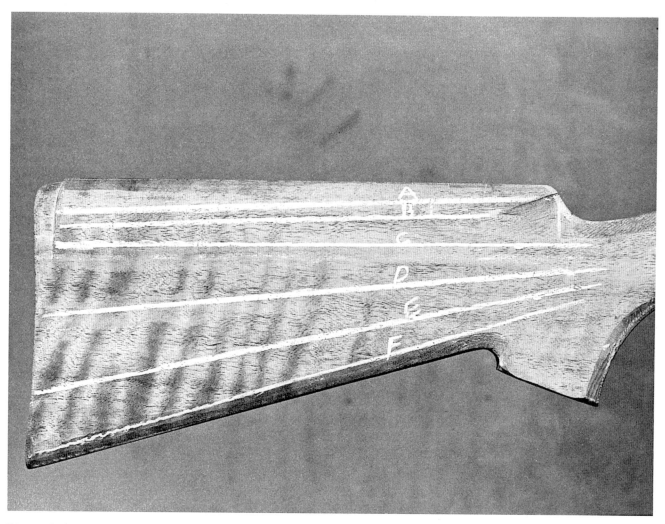

Figure 2-43

Shaping the Right Side of the Buttstock Between Lines B and E
Figures 2-44 and 2-45

This area is one of the easiest portions of the gunstock to shape as the stockmaker has two benchmarks, the width of the grip flat and the edge of the buttplate or pad, to work to or from. If you are planning to use a steel buttplate on the stock it must be inletted prior to this operation (see Appendix I). If you are going to use a rubber recoil pad, the outline of the pad should be traced on the butt of the stock.

Figures 2-44 and 2-45 illustrate the use of the 9-1/2-inch plane in removing the excess wood in this area. (The use and adjustments of the 9-1/2-inch plane are discussed in Figure 2-12.) This plane can be pushed straight forward for a wide cut, angled slightly and then pushed forward for a narrow cut, or pulled backward in either the angled or straight orientation depending on the location of the cut and the amount of wood that needs to be removed. The plane is held with the wrists in a semi-locked position and the stockmaker's forearms move in a plane parallel to the plane of the desired cut.

Follow the flow lines shown in Figure 2-43 and walk the plane around the stock in a series of fine cuts. It may be helpful if you add a third benchmark by planing the side of profile line (line D) down to almost finish dimensions first and then blend the wood from lines B and E in toward line D.

Compare Figure 2-44 to Figure 2-45. Note that there is more wood to be removed toward the grip than at the butt in this cut. To plane a taper you start at the end where the most wood has to be removed. Hold the plane at a slightly greater angle than the desired plane of the taper. Take short cuts at first and then gradually lower the angle of the plane until the cut runs the entire length of the taper.

Although you could use either the rasp or a wide file to shape this area of the stock, both of these tools leave compression marks below the surface of the wood which must be removed before the stock finish is applied. Sanding alone may or may not remove these compres-

Finish Shaping the Stock

Figure 2-44

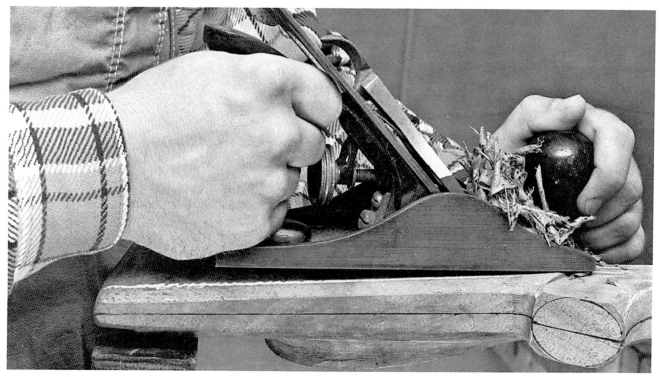

Figure 2-45

sion marks. In the author's opinion it is better to use a tool (the plane) that was designed for shaping smooth flat surfaces, than to try to rasp or file a flat surface 9 to 10 inches long.

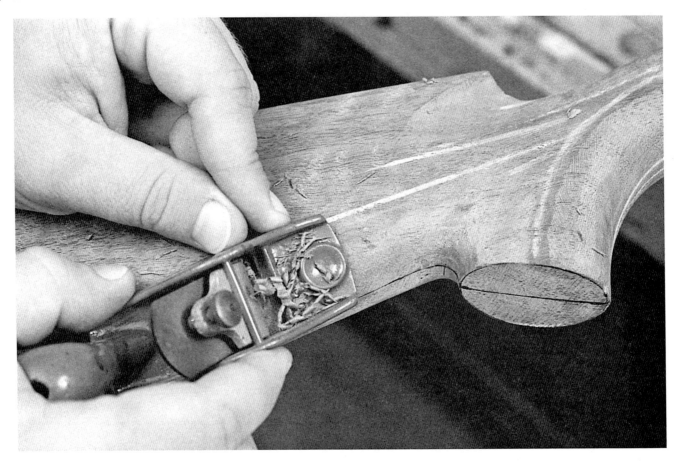

Figure 2-46

Shaping the Lower Right Side of the Buttstock and the Transitional Area Between the Side of the Butt and the Rear of the Pistol-Grip
Figures 2-46 through 2-48

The benchmarks for shaping the lower right side of the buttstock are the width at the butt (just above the toe) and the width of the grip. Follow the line flow diagram shown in Figure 2-43 and use the Nicholson 50 rasp, followed by the palm plane Figure 2-46, to shape the straight sides of the butt. Because the blade of the palm plane is located a short distance behind the nose of the plane, this tool will not reach all way to the rear of the grip. To shape the last 3/4-inch or so we will use the crossing file with a full drawfiling movement. As the file contacts the rear of the grip, rotate your hands upward and use the trailing edge of the file to blend the straight side of the butt into the curved sides of the grip as shown in Figure 2-47. Match the radius of the

Finish Shaping the Stock

Figure 2-47

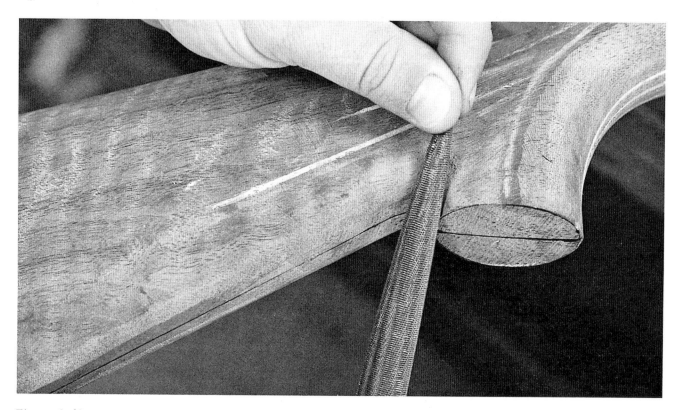

Figure 2-48

file to the radius of the shape being formed as shown in Figure 2-48.

Figure 2-49

Shaping the Toe-line of the Stock
Figures 2-49 and 2-50

The toe-line of the stock is shaped with the straight side of the square file as shown in Figure 2-49. Follow the line flow diagram, Figure 2-50, and gradually round over and blend the toe-line into the lower sides of the buttstock. Note that the cross-sectional shape of the toe-line directly behind the grip is shaped like a rounded "U" and that the cross section at the toe of the buttstock is more of a rounded "V" shape. Shape the toe-line accordingly.

Also see Figure 3-13 for more information on the shaping and sanding of the toe-line and Figures 2-53 and 2-54 for the selection and modification of this square file.

Finish Shaping the Stock

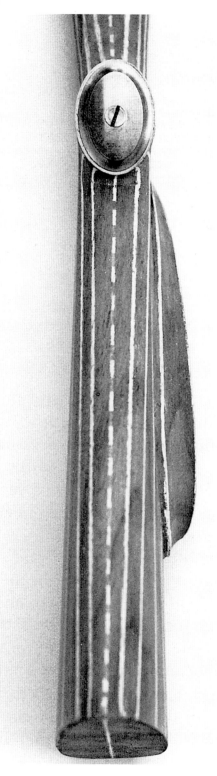

Figure 2-50

Line flow diagram of the toe-line of the buttstock.

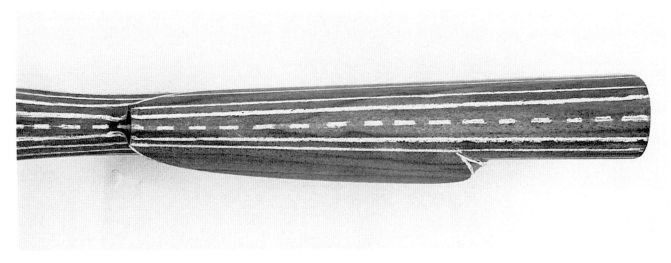

Figure 2-51

Shaping the Top and Sides of the Comb-line
Figures 2-51 and 2-52

The top and sides of the comb-line taper from the back to the front. Follow the line flow diagram shown in Figure 2-51.

The top and sides of the comb-line are shaped in a series of bevels as shown in Figure 2-52. The benchmarks for shaping this area are the centerline of the buttstock, the drop at the heel and comb, and the top of the cheekpiece molding. Note that line A in Figure 2-52 is located in the center of the first bevel. Care must be taken that the angle of this bevel is not too great or you will lose the very end of the cheekpiece molding.

After the initial bevels have been formed with the 9-1/2-inch plane, continue rounding and blending the top and sides over and down to line B on the right side of the buttstock. The area below line A on the left side of the stock requires a different shaping technique that will be discussed next.

Author's note: If the required drop at the heel and comb are known, and a steel buttplate installed, as in the case of Figure 2-52, the top of the comb can be shaped almost to final dimensions at this time. If these dimensions are not known, however, it is best to leave the comb-line heavy until the rest of the stock is shaped, and then gradually dress down both the comb-line and the cheekpiece until your eye aligns properly with the sights when the rifle is mounted naturally.

Finish Shaping the Stock

Figure 2-52

Shaping the Lower Left Side of the Buttstock
Figures 2-53 and 2-54

The first step in shaping the left side, the cheekpiece side of the stock, is to use a wax pencil to draw the rough shape of the desired cheekpiece onto the side of the buttstock. Next use the edge of a square rough cut file to file a small notch connecting the grip benchmark with the toe benchmark. This notch should follow Line E, Figure 2-55. Note, these files are available in most hardware stores. Take a straightedge with you and find one that has at least one perfectly flat side. Clip or grind off the last three to four inches of the taper, leaving a file approximately 9 inches long. Mark the flat side of the file. Place the flat side down and then make the right side of the file safe by grinding the teeth smooth with either a grinding wheel or belt sander. Place the safe side of the file toward the cheekpiece and round and blend the wood below line E from the toe to just behind the grip as shown in Figures 2-49 and 2-50. Use the lower right side of the buttstock as a pattern for this rounding and blending. Both sides should be the same.

The lower left rear of the grip is shaped and blended with the crossing file as discussed in Figure 2-47. This step can be done either now or after the wood directly in front of and below the cheekpiece is shaped.

Finish Shaping the Stock

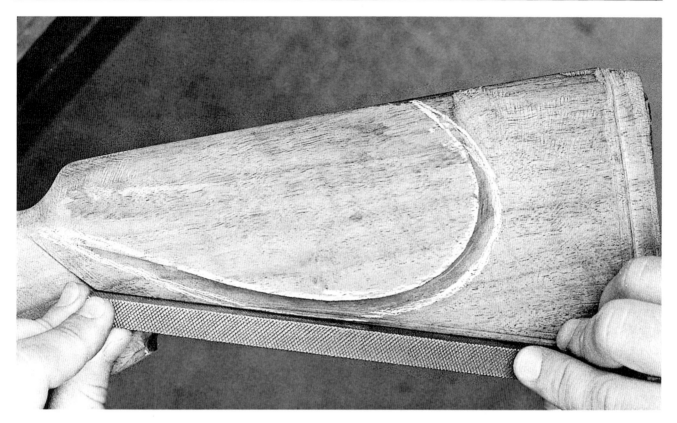

Figure 2-53

Figure 2-54

Professional Stockmaking

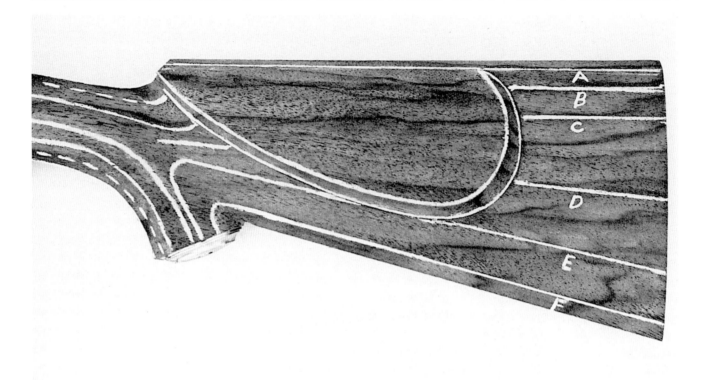

Figure 2-55

Shaping and Removal of Excess Wood Directly Behind the Cheekpiece
Figures 2-55 through 2-59

The left side of the buttstock is shaped along the flow lines shown in Figure 2-55. A straightedge placed along any of these lines should reveal a perfectly level (flat) surface. Note that line D extends into the pistol-grip of the stock.

The easiest way to shape behind the cheekpiece is to first drop a perpendicular line from the top of the buttstock extending from line A to line E, Figure 2-55. The majority of the excess wood is removed with the Nicholson 50 rasp Figure 2-56, followed by a wide smooth cut file Figure 2-57. Care must be taken to avoid creating any dips or bumps with the rasp or file and the surface should be frequently checked for level by laying the straightedge along each of the flow lines.

The benchmarks for shaping this area are the shape of the buttplate or pad and the taper on the *right* side of the buttstock. Both sides of the buttstock should have the same

Figure 2-56

taper from the back to the front. The easiest check for this is to simply hold the stock at arm's length. Any difference in the tapers should be readily apparent to the eyes. This is one area of shaping where many otherwise good stockmakers fall flat. If the tapers on both sides of the stock are not the same, it looks like hell. Take your time and do it right. Another check for the taper

Figure 2-57

on the left side of the stock is done with a cutout straightedge placed along line D as shown in Figure 2-58.

The finish shaping of the area is shown in Figure 2-59. The small triangles of wood at the top rear and bottom rear of the cheekpiece will be shaped next.

Finish Shaping the Stock

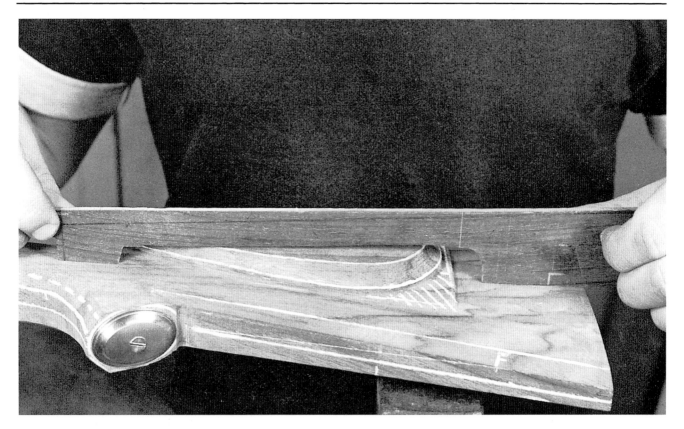

Figure 2-58

Figure 2-59

Figure 2-60

Outlining the Ghostline Cheekpiece
Figures 2-60 and 2-61

Chisels have a limited use in the shaping of the stock. However, in those places where they are used they do the job better then any other tool. Figures 2-60 and 2-61 illustrate the use of the modified deep mortice chisel and the 1-1/4-inch paring chisel in outlining the ghost-line of the cheekpiece.

Most semi-inletted and shaped stocks come with a cheekpiece whose side bevel is radiused into the side of the buttstock. In order to change this type of cheekpiece into a ghost-line cheekpiece it is necessary to define and outline the edge of the cheekpiece.

The first step in this process is to draw the rough shape of the desired cheekpiece on to the side of the stock with a wax pencil. (Make the outlines fairly wide at this point to allow for the final detail shaping which comes later.) Next, we will use the modified deep mortice chisel to lightly score a line around

FINISH SHAPING THE STOCK

Figure 2-61

the outside of the wax pencil outline as shown in Figure 2-60. The right hand provides a slight downward pressure to the chisel, while the fingers of the left hand both guide, steady, and push the tool around the perimeter. For outlining such as this, only the rear or trailing portion of the blade is used to make the cut. Using only a portion of the blade allows us to better follow the curves. Also see Figure 2-25 for alternative tools used to make this cut.

The 1-1/4-inch paring chisel is next used to form the initial shelf or ledge of the ghostline as shown in Figure 2-61. In use, the tool is slid sideways parallel to the line flow of the stock. Use light cuts only. Trying to remove too much wood at once may result in the tearing and pulling of the fibers instead of the clean cut we are after.

This technique of outlining and paring can also be used to remove the excess wood and rough shape the area directly to the front and below the front of the cheekpiece. Also see Figures 2-54, 2-71 through 2-73.

Shaping and Blending the Triangle of Wood Directly Behind and Below the Cheekpiece
Figures 2-62 through 2-65

This area is shaped and blended into the line flow of the buttstock with the Nicholson 50 rasp followed by the wide smooth cut file. The rasp and the file are used both in the modified and straight forward, or normal, drawfiling movements and care must be taken to follow the correct line flow of the buttstock. The modified drawfiling technique with the rasp is illustrated in Figures 2-62 and 2-63. The rasp is held at a slight angle to the line flow being rasped. Push the rasp forward along the line flow while at the same time pushing the tool obliquely in order to present clean teeth for the most efficient cutting action of the tool. Using this technique allows you to remove the wood quickly while still being able to control the correct line flow of the stock.

Work slowly and carefully here. Do not be tempted to place the rasp or file flat on the surface of the stock and file or rasp with a straight ahead movement following the curvature of the cheekpiece. Filing a curved surface at an angle to the line flow will result in a dipping of the leading edge of the tool and a subsequent dip in the surface of the stock. Dips in these areas require major surgery and a lot of reshaping of the tapers on both sides of the stock to correct, *if they can be corrected at all.*

The straightforward or normal drawfiling technique is illustrated in Figures 2-64 and 2-65. The tool is held at a slight angle to the line flow and then pushed forward, but not obliquely, along the line flow.

Finish Shaping the Stock

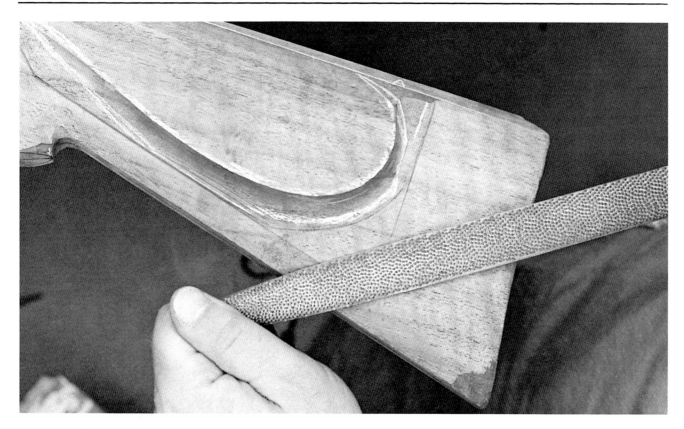

Figure 2-62

Figure 2-63

Figure 2-64

Figure 2-65

Figure 2-66

Shaping the Small Triangle of Wood Directly Behind and Above the Cheekpiece
Figure 2-66

Due to the small size of the area of wood that needs to be removed from behind the upper portion of the cheekpiece it may be impractical to remove the excess wood using the modified drawfiling technique alone. In this instance straight-ahead filing may be necessary for roughing in the area only. The stockmaker must use extreme care however and be well aware of the tendency of the leading edge of the file to dip downward. The finish shaping is best done with the modified palm plane shown in Figure 2-66. Angle the plane slightly so that the blade will reach right up to the edge of the cheekpiece and then push the plane straight ahead along the flow lines. Note that because of its short base this plane has a tendency to dip slightly into the wood. It should therefore only be used for short cuts such as this. The curls of wood up against the cheekpiece are removed with the modified deep mortice and paring chisels as discussed in Figures 2-60 and 2-61.

Shaping the Ghostline of the Cheekpiece
Figures 2-67 through 2-70

Over the past 60 — 70 years, the shape of the classic bolt action riflestock has evolved into a rigidly structured line-form in which every line or shape contributes to either the structural stability of the stock or the functional qualities of the rifle. Therein lies the beauty of the classic stock. Every aspect of its form contributes to its function. Such design constraints, however, allow little room for artistic expression on the part of the individual stockmaker.

The one area of the stock where these constraints do not apply is the shape of the cheekpiece, and many stockmakers have developed distinctive cheekpieces that are almost signatures to their work. Stocks by Griffin and Howe, Tom Shelhamer, Dale Goens, and Al Beisen are instantly recognizable. The cheekpiece shown in the Sanding Section (Book III) contains elements of the author's design that as of yet have not been copied. (The pancake cheekpiece with a drop-ledge to the bottom of the fluting is a bear to shape and worse yet to finish. Those of you who would like to use this design are more than welcome to do so.) In addition, every stockmaker has particular styles of cheekpieces that they feel most comfortable using or think look better than the other styles. There are many choices available. Use the one that looks best to you and then try to shape it as gracefully as possible.

Figures 2-67 through 2-70 illustrate the square file (*safe side down*) shaping the cheekpiece ghostline. Develop this line slowly, as any flat spot on the curvature will require the changing of the entire curve to fix.

Finish Shaping the Stock

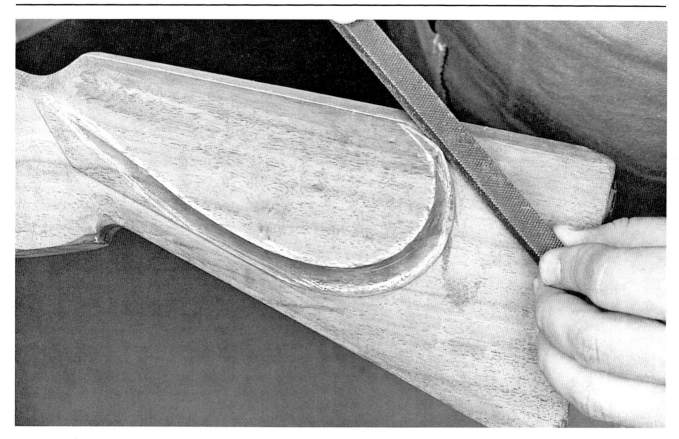

Figure 2-67

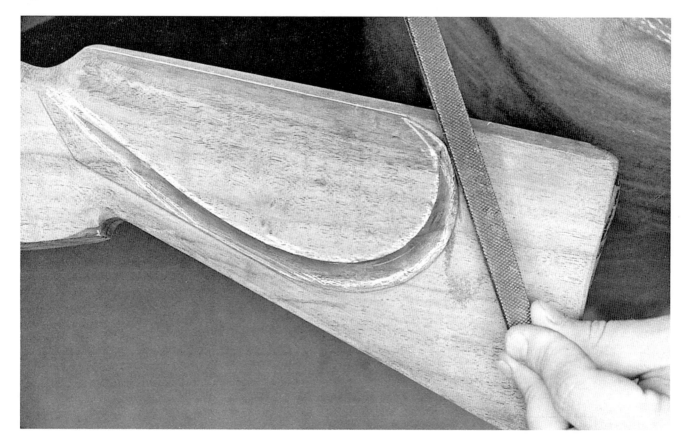

Figure 2-68

Professional Stockmaking

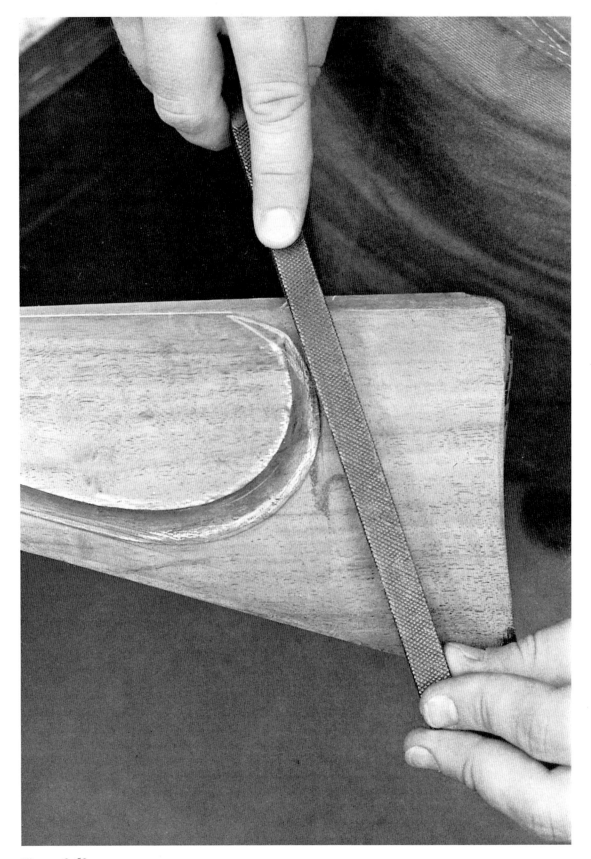

Figure 2-69

Finish Shaping the Stock

Figure 2-70

Shaping the Area Between the Front of the Cheekpiece and the Rear of the Grip
Figures 2-71 through 2-73

Earlier in the text it was stated that there is *no set* sequence of the steps that took the stock from rough shaped to finish shape. Rather, each area must be gradually shaped and blended with its adjacent line flows. Figure 2-49, shows the square file being used to shape the toe-line and lower sides of the buttstock. Is that particular photo out of sequence? Figures 2-71 through 2-73 seem to bear this out in that the cheekpiece side of the stock is being worked on *before* the lower left side of the butt has been finished shaped. Was this a mistake? No! On this particular stock it was simply easier to shape the side first and then go back and shape and blend the toe-line and lower grip into the side. Each stock will differ slightly in the shaping sequences, but in general it is best to first rough shape those areas of the stock that need the most wood removed and then blend in those areas that are closer to the final shape.

In Figure 2-71, the crossing file is used to shape the lower rear of the grip. This area is best shaped using a normal draw-filing motion. To shape and blend the side of the stock into the back of the grip simply rotate your wrists upward at the end of the drawfiling stroke.

Finish Shaping the Stock

Figure 2-71

Professional Stockmaking

Figure 2-72

Turn back to Figure 2-54 for a minute. Note the triangle of excess wood between the front of the cheekpiece and the grip. This excess wood was first removed and the area rough shaped with the deep mortice chisel and paring chisel technique described in Figures 2-60 and 2-61.

Figure 2-73

Figures 2-72 and 2-73 show the use of the crossing file in the finish shaping of the area of wood between the cheekpiece and the rear of the grip. Follow the flowlines shown in Figure 2-55 and use only the trailing edge of the crossing file in the normal drawfiling technique to finish shape this area. Note that the movement of the file was a straight sideways push from the edge of the cheekpiece toward the rear of the grip.

Professional Stockmaking

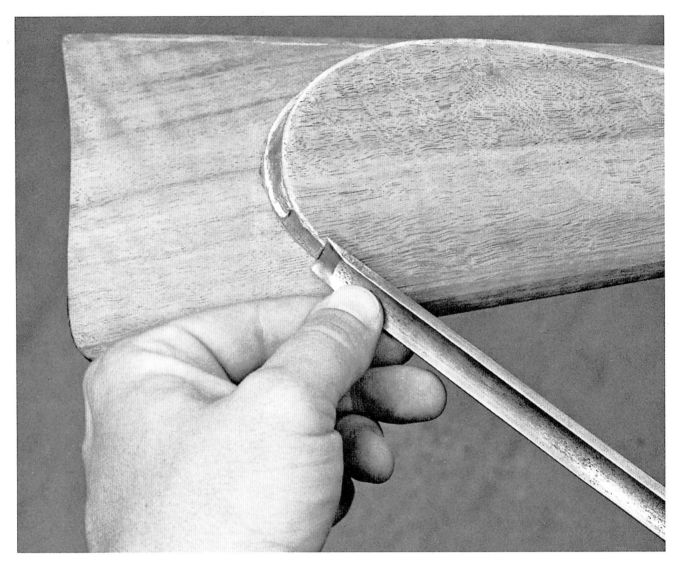

Figure 2-74

Shaping the Radius on the Side of the Cheekpiece
Figures 2-74 through 2-76

The radius on the side of the cheekpiece is shaped with various size in-cannel gouges, Figure 2-74, and barrel channel rasps Figures 2-75 and 2-76. Both hands are used to steady and guide the tools.

Care must be taken when using the rasps so that the teeth on the bottom of the rasp do not scratch the side of the stock. Figure 2-76 illustrates the end point of the rasp's usefulness. The radius on each end of the cheekpiece is best shaped with the in-cannel gouges.

Finish Shaping the Stock

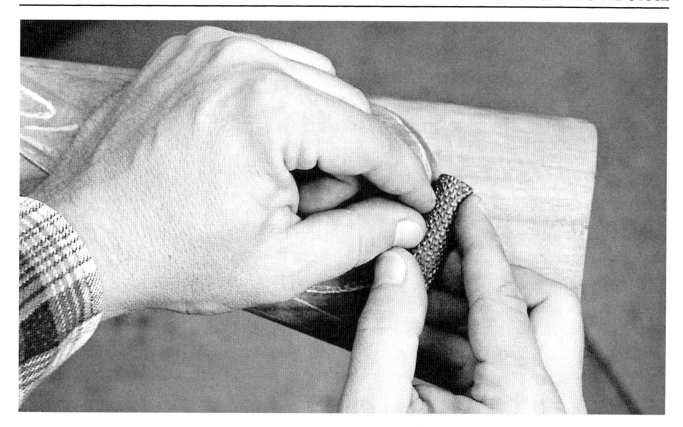

Figure 2-75

Figure 2-76

Rough Shaping the Comb Nose Fluting, the Top and Upper Sides of the Wrist
Section 5
Shaping the Wrist and Comb Nose Fluting
Figures 2-77 through 2-84

The purpose of the fluting is to provide a recessed, or concave area, to accommodate and support the fleshy portion of the base of the thumb when a "thumb across the top of the wrist" grip is used to hold the rifle. If the Springfield "thumb alongside" hold is used, the fluting plays very little functional role in holding the rifle and then has purely esthetic value in the overall lines of the stock.

The angle of the top line of the fluting, and hence the amount of wood that needs to be removed, will vary according to the action being stocked, or more specifically to the shape of the tang on the action being stocked.

The tangs on Mauser and Sako actions are narrow and straight sided and therefore do not dictate the shape or the taper of the top and sides of the wrist. To accommodate the slimmer wrists found on most Mauser or Sako rifles the angle of the top of the flute should extend from just below the nose of the comb to a point even with or slightly above the toe of the stock.

On Model 70 Winchester and Springfield actions the wide cloverleaf shaped tang dictates a wider cross-section to the wrist. On stocks for these actions the fluting line should extend from just below the nose of the comb to a point approximately 1 inch above the toe of the stock. This slightly higher angle allows you to remove slightly more wood from the fluting in order to accommodate the wider top of the wrist dictated by the width of the tang.

Although such a small change of angles may seem insignificant at first glance, they are not. It is the small changes, better yet the understanding of how the small changes affect the overall handling qualities of the rifle, that make the difference between a rifle that handles well and points naturally and one that feels and points like a club.

Finish Shaping the Stock

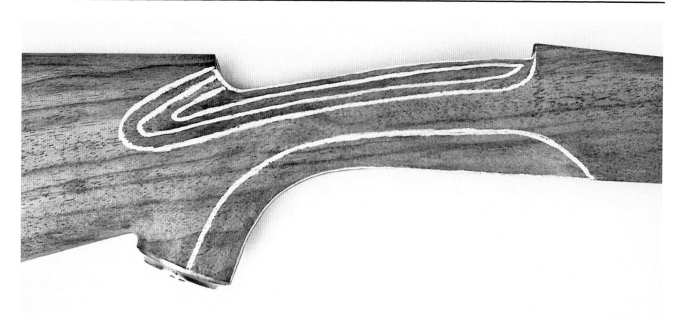

Figure 2-77

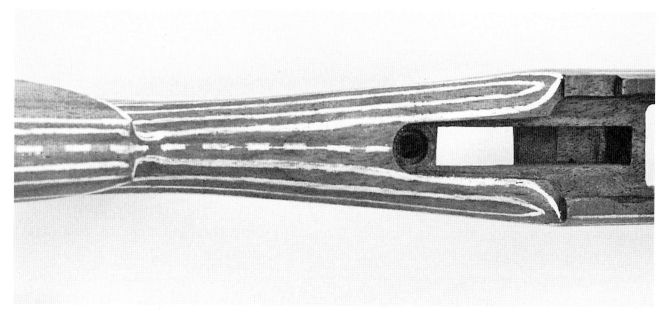

Figure 2-78

Figures 2-77 and 2-78 are the line flow diagrams for the sides and top of the wrist. Note that the line forming the top of the fluting curves around the back of the flute and then flows forward to the back of the receiver. This line delineates the top from the sides of the wrist. Also see Figure 2-59 which illustrates the line flow diagram of the cheekpiece side of a stock using a Griffin and Howe-style cheekpiece, and Figure 3-20 (in Sanding Section) for the line flow diagrams of a stock using the "American classic" style of cheekpiece.

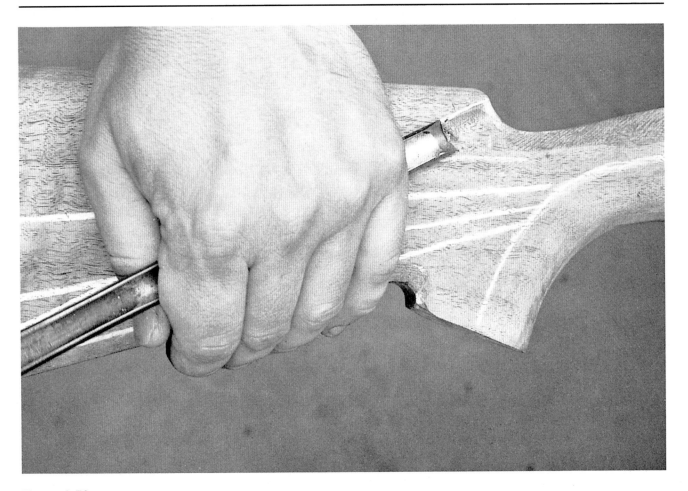

Figure 2-79

The fluting at the nose of the comb is rough shaped using the in-cannel gouges as shown in Figures 2-79 through 2-81. A push/pull muscle control is used to prevent any slip of the chisel from traveling too far forward and possibly damaging another area of the stock. The direction of the cut, and all cutting forces involved, come from the angle formed by the right hand/wrist alignment and a straightforward movement of the right forearm. The left hand both steadies and positions the tool.

In Figure 2-79, note the alignment of the in-cannel gouge with the top line of the flute. The top line of the flute should be perfectly straight and the in-cannel gouge is the best tool that the author has found for this particular job. With the exception of the top line of the flute, the gouge is used primarily for the gross removal of excess wood from the flute. The rough shaping of the majority of the flute will be done with the Nicholson 50 rasp followed by the "O" cut crossing file. See Figures 2-82 through 2-88.

Finish Shaping the Stock

Figure 2-80

Figure 2-81

Figure 2-82

In Figures 2-82 and 2-83, the curved side of the Nicholson 50 rasp is used to smooth out the chisel marks left by the in-cannel gouge and also to rough shape and blend the rear and lower boundaries of the flute and the side of the wrist. The trailing edge of the rasp is used in the modified drawfiling motion following the flow lines shown in Figure 2-77. To shape the curvature of the back and lower fluting rotate the rasp forward slightly using the left hand as a pivot point. Continue this movement with the curved side of the rasp forward to approximately the point shown in Figure 2-83 and then flip the rasp over and use the flat side to gradually shape and round over the top and upper side of the wrist as shown in Figure 2-84. The flat side of the rasp is again used in the modified drawfiling motion following the line flow diagrams shown in Figures 2-77 and 2-78.

Because the rasp removes a lot of wood very quickly, this tool must be used very slowly and carefully for the rough shaping of these areas. The finish shaping of the fluting and top and sides of the wrist will be done with the crossing file discussed in the next step.

Finish Shaping the Stock

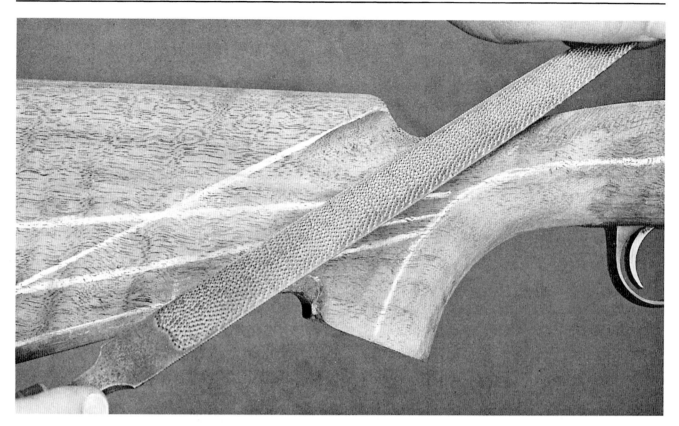

Figure 2-83

Figure 2-84

Figure 2-85

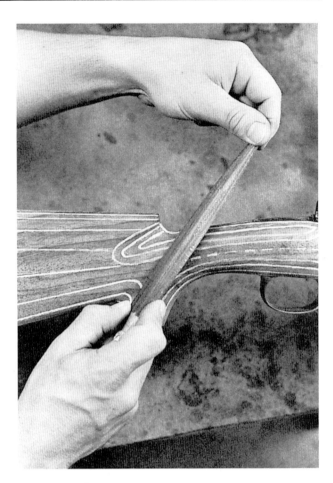

Figure 2-86

Finish Shaping of the Comb Nose Fluting, the Top and Upper Sides of the Wrist
Figures 2-85 through 2-88

The fluting, and the top and upper sides of the wrist, are finish shaped with the trailing edge of the crossing file as shown in Figures 2-85 through 2-88. This file is used in the modified drawfiling motion, pivoting the file around the fingers of the left hand to shape the curvature at the back of the flute and the lower boundary line of the upper wrist. Follow the line flow diagrams, Figure 2-77 and 2-78, and continue this drawfiling movement forward to gradually round, shape, and blend the top and upper sides of the wrist. To shape the little curve between the top and sides of the wrist at the rear of the action, simply rotate your wrists upward at the end of the draw filing movement as shown in Figure 2-88.

Finish Shaping the Stock

Figure 2-87

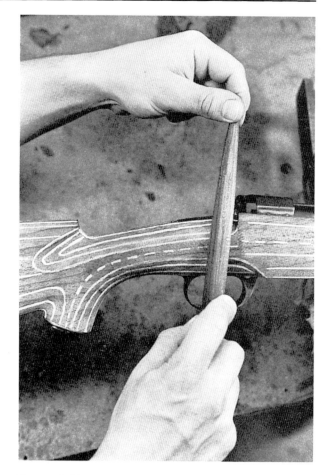

Figure 2-88

The top of the wrist should be well rounded in cross-section. To maintain and shape this "roundness" it is often helpful to work from the top of the wrist downward toward the sides. Working from the opposite direction, from the sides upward toward the top of the wrist, tends to flatten this curve. It is the mark of a good craftsman that both sides of the wrist be symmetrical. This is entirely possible. It just takes patience and careful work with the crossing file. Review Figure 2-78. Note how the lines on both sides of the wrist are identical.

Shaping the Pistol-Grip and Finger Clearance Arch
Figures 2-89 through 2-97

The purpose of the pistol-grip/wrist area of the stock is to position the shooter's wrist, hand, and trigger finger in such a way that it provides easy access to the trigger; comfortably and securely supports the hand; and allows a quick, natural pointability of the rifle. As such, it is one of the most important areas of the stock in terms of the function of the rifle in the field.

The factors that affect the size, shape, and positioning of the pistol-grip were discussed in Figures 2-5 and 2-6, but will also be briefly reviewed here. The size of the shooter's hand and the position he holds his forearm and elbow, relative to the ground, will determine the depth of the grip and also the radius of its front curvature. The type of hold that the shooter uses, the "thumb across the top of the wrist" or "thumb alongside the wrist," affects both the curvature of the grip and also the positioning of the nose of the comb.

Through practice in mounting the rifle one can adapt to a stock that is either too long or too short, or whose drop at the heel or comb just isn't quiet right - but a stock whose grip feels like a club, will handle like a club period, regardless of what other dimensions are correct.

Sounds complicated? It is. Fortunately however, once the size and positioning of the grip have been determined, the shaping and blending of the curves and lines of this area are relatively easy to do. Slow and careful removal of wood, coupled with many repeated grippings and practice mountings are all that is necessary. Trust your hands and fingers to show you where more wood has to be removed. Running your fingers over an area that looks smooth will often reveal bumps or valleys that need attention and blending. Trust your sense of touch, and simply shape what feels best to your hand.

Slow and careful blending of line flows is the key to good shaping. Never attempt to shape any one area in its entirety, but rather blend each area into the others until the whole slowly comes to life.

Finish Shaping the Stock

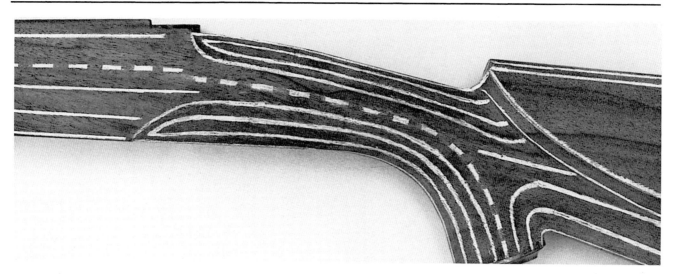

Figure 2-89

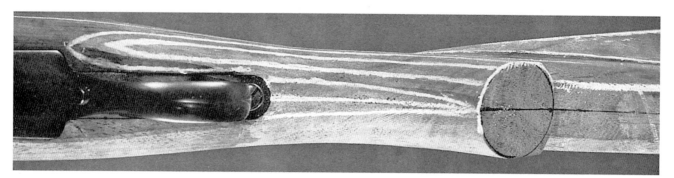

Figure 2-90

Figure 2-91

Figures 2-89 through 2-91 illustrate the line flow diagrams of the grip and finger clearance arch of the stock.

Figure 2-92 *Figure 2-93*

The front and lower sides of the pistol-grip are rough shaped with the Nicholson 50 rasp as shown in Figures 2-92 and 2-93. Both the flat side and the curved side of the rasp are used in this procedure. The flat side is used for the gross removal of excess wood from the grip. The trailing edge of the curved side is then used to smooth and further define the shape of the grip. Both sides of the rasp use the modified drawfiling motion with the right arm advancing the rasp forward, while the left hand pushes the rasp sideways in an archlike movement pivoting on the right hand. Use light cuts and gradually round the grip by using a series of flats that approximate the flow lines shown in Figures 2-89 through 2-91. Leave the grip heavy at this stage, as the final shaping, rounding, and blending will be done with the crossing file.

Finish Shaping the Stock

Figure 2-94

Figure 2-95

Note the modified drawfiling technique used with the crossing file in Figures 2-94 and 2-95. Pivoting the file around the right hand allows the trailing edge of the file to follow the flow lines of the grip with little effort on the stockmaker's part.

Leave the side profiling lines of the grip flat for now. (The side profiling line is the solid center line running from the center of the grip-cap upward through the center of the wrist. See Figure 2-89.) Later, after we have rough shaped the finger clearance arch, we will come back and "bell in" (concave) the sides of the grip slightly to provide a better purchase for the shooter's hand. What we are after is a consistent and positive positioning of the shooter's hand on the grip.

Figure 2-96   Figure 2-97

Concaving the sides of the pistol-grip slightly allows the shooter's hand/slide back to a natural and comfortable position that is reproducible from one shot to the next. This allows the shooter's trigger finger and wrist to form consistent angles to the rifle which in turn is conducive to quick handling and pointability of the rifle. A totally straight sided grip, or a grip that tapers toward the grip-cap, causes the shooter's hand to slide downward during recoil and necessitates the realignment of the shooter's hand and wrist between shots.

The concaving of the sides of the grip (more properly the tapering and flaring of the grip) need not be much, 1/8- to 3/16-inch is generally sufficient. The taper starts at the grip-cap, flows inward along the sides of the grip to a point just forward of the nose of the comb, and then flares outward to blend into the sides of the wrist.

Figures 2-96 and 2-97 illustrate the finish shaping of the finger clearance arch. The finger clearance arch, as its name implies, provides clearance for the shooter's trigger finger to reach the trigger. In addition to fulfilling its primary function, this arch also provides a pleasing architectural line flow whose curved sides allow for a more efficient rounding of the transitional area between the front of the lower wrist and the curved front and sides of the pistol-grip.

This arch begins just to the rear of the floorplate and sweeps upward and back to blend into the flow lines of the sides of the wrist. On the bottom it sweeps in toward the trigger guard, runs almost parallel to the guard bow and blends into the front and sides of the pistol-grip.

Note the trail of wood filings in Figure 2-97. These indicate the file's area of contact with the wood and also its direction of travel. Push the wood in front of the file as if you were molding a piece of clay. Take your time and use both your fingers and eyes to detect any bumps or hollows that need further shaping and blending.

The sides of the finger clearance arch are slightly rounded in cross-section. It is often easier to establish and maintain this curvature by starting at the bottom edge of the arch and gradually shaping and rounding upward. If you start at the top and work downward there will be a tendency to use too much angle on the file and flatten the sides of the arch, which will make it difficult to blend the sides and bottom of the arch into the wrist and pistol-grip.

The concept of the finger clearance arch was initially developed by the stockmakers at Griffin and Howe in the 1930s. The Griffin and Howe arch, however, left much to be desired both architecturally and aesthetically since the sides were almost flat and the arch rose almost vertically from just in front of the guard bow. The author's version of the finger clearance arch, which was introduced to the custom gun trade in 1981 and is currently used by many custom stockmakers, not only extends the front of the arch forward to obtain a more esthetically pleasing line flow, but also rounds the sides of the arch to structurally re-inforce and strengthen the area of the stock on either side of the trigger mortice of the stock inletting.

Professional Stockmaking

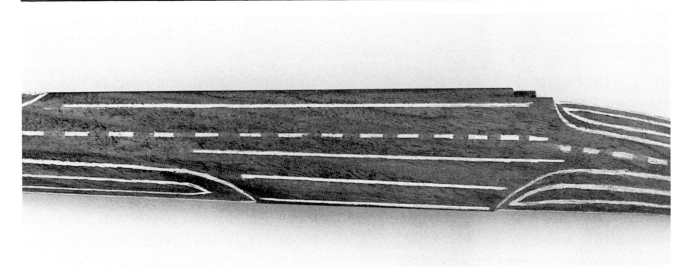

Figure 2-98

Shaping the Body of the Stock Through the Receiver Area
Section 6
Shaping the Body and Forearm of the Stock
Figures 2-98 and 2-99

The shaping of the body of the stock is perhaps the simplest shaping on the entire stock in that it consists entirely of straight, tapered line flows.

There are two basic shapes or profiles through the body of the stock: the first is a straight taper from the rear of the receiver extending all the way to the end of the forearm tip; the second is a straight taper from the rear of the receiver to the front of the receiver, followed by a second taper that extends to the end of the forearm. To the author's eye the second option looks best as it imparts a sense of directed movement to the line flow of the stock and separates the body and the forearm of the stock as individual entities.

The body of the stock is shaped almost entirely with the 9-1/2 inch smooth plane, angled slightly as discussed in Figure 2-15, and following the line flows shown in Figure 2-98. Note that the line flow above the profile line runs almost parallel to the top of the stock, and that the line flow below the profile line runs upward slightly from the back to the front. Use the straight edge to check that these lines are perfectly flat. The contour gauge, Figure 2-99, is

Finish Shaping the Stock

Figure 2-99

used to confirm that both sides of the stock are symmetrical.

During the shaping of the body of the stock, draw perpendicular lines with a wax pencil at the front of the front receiver ring and just forward of the finger clearance arch at the back of the receiver. These lines provide a constant reminder of the end points of the tapers of the body of the stock and are also used as reference points at which to check the symmetry of the contours of the stock.

The stock illustrated measures 1.975 inches wide at the rear ring of the receiver and 1.875 inches wide at the front ring for a taper back to front of 0.100 inch. These measurements, of course, must be proportional to the overall size of the rifle. Care must be taken not to get the width at the front ring too narrow. You must have enough wood to gently round over the sides of the stock. The body of the stock is widest at the profile line which is represented by broken lines in Figure 2-98.

Do not cut the ejection port at this time. The extra wood left in this area helps support the sole of the plane and the sanding block, allowing us to more easily shape and maintain the straight line flow on the right upper side of the stock. The ejection port will be cut in after the stock has been finish shaped *and* sanded.

Profiling the Bottom and Sides of the Forearm
Figures 2-100 and 2-101

The size and shape of the forearm are determined by its length, the bottom and side profile lines, and by the cross-sectional shape at the tip of the forearm. In the author's opinion, a forearm between 9-10" looks best on rifles with 22-24" barrels. On rifles with 26" barrels a forearm of 11-12" looks about right. This is a matter of personal tastes however, and you should use whatever length forearm looks best to you.

The first step in shaping the forearm is to determine its desired depth and width at the end of the forearm tip. On sporter rifles a forearm that is almost round in cross-section feels best to the author's hands. In general, the author's forearms start out one-tenth inch (1/10") wider than they are deep and are adjusted from there.

The bottom profile line of the forearm can be treated in several ways. If a shallow depth at the tip is desired, the bottom profile line can be tapered upward from the front tang of the guard to whatever depth is desired at the tip. The treatment works well if a very short (7- or 8- inch) forearm is desired. A good example of this can be seen in the styling of the pre-war German and English sporter stocks.

The second treatment, and the one the author thinks looks best and therefore uses most often, is to simply continue the taper established by the back to front slope of the trigger guard assembly all the way to the front of the forearm tip.

Most commercial Mauser guards, and those made by metalsmith Ted Blackburn have a seven degree back-to-front slope that allows for a forearm deep enough for most light to moderately recoiling rifles. For the heavier recoiling rifles, however, the author prefers the guards by Pete Greisel whose four degree bottom taper allows for a deeper and heavier forearm.

The side profiling lines of the forearm can either be a continuation of the side profiling lines of the body of the stock, or a straight taper from the front ring of the action to the end of the forearm. On varmint or bench rest rifles the author prefers to use the former

Finish Shaping the Stock

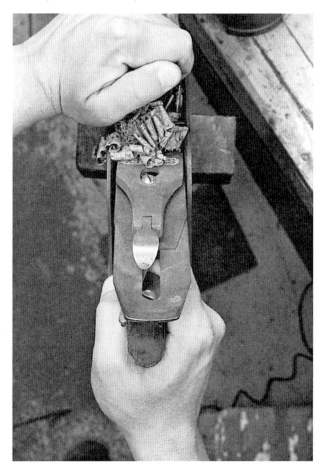

Figure 2-100

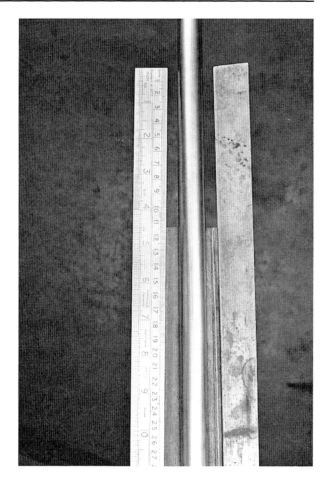

Figure 2-101

single taper; on sporter stocks the author prefers to use the latter or double taper technique.

The side profiling lines of the forearm are planed with either the 9-1/2-inch smooth plane or the 24-inch jointer plane and the bottom profile line of the forearm is planed down with the 9-1/2-inch plane illustrated in Figure 2-100. A straightedge is then used to confirm that these lines are truly smooth and flat. No bumps or dips in these lines, please.

The tapers of the side profiling lines must be the same on both sides of the forearm. Figure 2-101 illustrates the method used to check the symmetry of the tapers. A straightedge is placed on the profiling line on each side of the forearm and extended past the tip of the stock. If the edge of each straightedge is equidistant from the side of the barrel, the tapers on both sides of the forearm are equal.

Professional Stockmaking

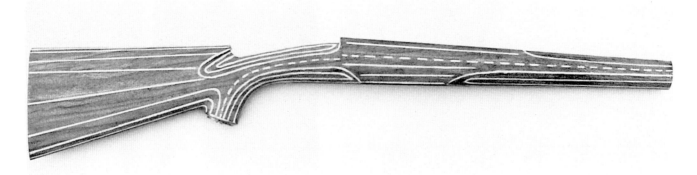

Figure 2-102

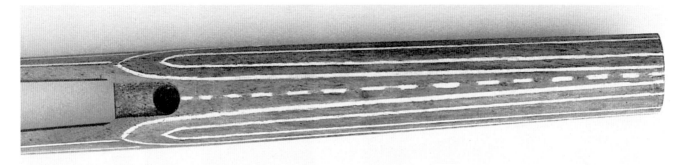

Figure 2-103

Rough Shaping the Forearm
Figures 2-102 through 2-105

The sides and bottom of the forearm have some of the longest, straight, flat line flows of the entire stock. Because of the length involved it is very easy to leave bumps or dips along the flow lines that should be flat. A straightedge placed along the flow lines shown in Figures 2-102 and 2-103 will reveal any areas that need further attention. A visual inspection, squinting down the forearm from the tip toward the trigger guard, will also reveal any bumps or dips which can then be smoothed out with either file or plane.

If you have ordered the stock fully shaped, the forearm may only need minor attention from the planes and files to true-up and smooth its surface. If, however, you have ordered the stock oversize though the forearm, then the forearm is rough shaped with the 9-1/2-inch smooth plane using bevel cuts as shown in Figures 2-104 and 2-105. Note that the cross-sectional shape of the forearm tip has been drawn on the end of the stock and also that a center line has been added on the tip and underside of the forearm to aid in the shaping of the forearm.

Finish Shaping the Stock

Figure 2-104

Figure 2-105

Figure 2-106

Finish Shaping the Forearm
Figures 2-106 through 2-110

The curved fillets on either side of the front tang of the trigger guard are shaped with a flicking motion of the crossing file, Figure 2-106. The straight line flows of the lower sides and bottom of the bottom of the forearm are brought to their final shape using both the 9-1/2-inch smooth plane and the smaller palm plane shown in Figure 2-107.

For the best control in the shaping of these straight line flows it is important that after every couple of passes with the plane you rotate the stock slightly in the vise so that the line flow being planed is most easily accessible. Try to make both sides of the forearm symmetrical throughout. It isn't hard to do. Slow and careful work and a lot of patience are all that is required. Shape a line flow on one side and then rotate the stock in the vise and shape that same line flow on the other side of the forearm. Use your eyes and also the pattern-maker gauge (Figure 2-99) to check the symmetry of both sides. Any minor bumps or differences between the two sides can be corrected with the plane or by drawfiling the area with a wide smooth cut file.

Finish Shaping the Stock

Figure 2-107

Figure 2-108

The rounded bevels at the top of the forearm are rough shaped in two stages with the Nicholson 50 rasp used in a straightforward rasping motion. The first bevel is shown in Figures 2-108 and 2-109. The top edge of this bevel follows the contour of the barrel, leaving a flat shelf about 1/8-inch wide on both sides of the barrel channel. The second roughing bevel extends from the white line to the pencil line shown in Figure 2-110. The fillet at the rear of these bevels is shaped and blended with the crossing file. The finish shaping and rounding of these bevels is accomplished by drawfiling with the wide, smooth-cut file.

Finish Shaping the Stock

Figure 2-109

Figure 2-110

Shaping the Ejection Port and Bolt Handle Recess
Figures 2-111 through 2-112

The author prefers to not "cut in" either the ejection port or the bolt handle recess until after the stock is completely sanded. The wood in the port helps support the sanding block and aids in sanding this area perfectly flat and smooth. In order to maintain the continuity of the shaping section however, this section is included here. **SAND THE STOCK FIRST!!**

The ejection port is cut in two steps. In the first step, a 1/4-inch chain-saw file is used to cut through the wood at each end of the ejection port. This cut should be perpendicular to the action and extend down to the depth of the ejection port of the action. The wood between these cuts is then removed with the chisels, rasps, or files depending on the cuttability of the wood.

In the second step, the chain-saw file is used to angle the ends of the cut downward. The distance down depends in part on the overall size of the rifle through the body of the stock and in part on personal preference. The inside edge of this cut should come no closer than 1/32-inch from the bottom of the ejection port in the action.

The bottom of these angled cuts are then connected with a pencil line and a medium width file is used to file a flat bevel extending from the pencil line upward and inward leaving a narrow flat ledge of wood between the action and the ejection port bevel. The finished ejection port is shown in Figure 2-111.

Figure 2-112 illustrates the finish inletting of the bolt handle recess. This recess is "cut in" by coating the bottom and sides of the bolt handle with inletting black, noting the areas of contact, and then using the No. 5 sweep 8mm and the No. 9 sweep 7mm gouge to remove the appropriate areas of wood. Repeat this process until the bolt closes fully and a small amount of clearance (0.020") exists between the bolt handle and the surrounding wood of the recess.

Finish Shaping the Stock

This rifle was chambered for a .50 cal. wildcat cartridge formed by necking up a .460 Weatherby. Double square bridge magnum length action. Huge rifle! Weight 15-1/2 lbs, length of pull almost 16". Owner used it to pole-ax a Cape buffalo - one shot at 30 yards.

Figure 2-112

Professional Stockmaking

Of all of the photographs in the sanding section, Figure 3-1 best illustrates the book's subtitle Through the Eyes of a Stockmaker.

BOOK III

SANDING AND STOCK FINISHING
Section 1 - Sanding

The purpose of sanding is to provide a smooth and uniform surface on which to apply the stock finish. This is accomplished through the use of various grades, or grits, of abrasive paper supported by shaped blocks or backers. The backer provides uniform support to the sandpaper so that it will grind the wood to a true and level surface, free of all tool marks, small dips and bumps.

There are two phases involved in sanding a stock, the rough sanding and the finish sanding. The rough sanding using grits 150, 180, 220, and 280, removes a relatively large amount of wood in the leveling and truing-up of the stock and care must be taken to avoid changing the shape of the stock or the rounding over of any sharp edges. Sand only enough with each grit to remove any surface defects or scratches left by the previous grade of sandpaper. In theory, once the surface of the stock has been leveled, and any and all tool marks have been removed by the coarse grits of paper, you should only have to remove an amount of wood from the surface equal to the depth of the deepest scratch marks left by the preceding grit paper. In actual practice we will remove that much plus a little more.

The second phase of sanding is the "finish" sanding during which very little wood is removed from the surface. Finish sanding uses grits of 320, 400, 500, 600, and up to 1200 and 1500 to polish the surface of the wood. These finer grits are also used to "cut back" the stock finish applied during the pore filling operation and to smooth the surface of the finish in preparation for additional coats.

Before we get to the actual sanding operations, it may help if we know a little more about the physical composition of wood. Wood consists of vascular bundles of fiber whose cell walls are made of lignin and cellulose. The pores you see in wood are the open ends of vessels that were used to transport water and nutrients throughout the tree during its lifetime. When the tree is cut, or dies, these vessels dry up, shrink, and harden to a degree, but each individual cell, or vascular bundle, remains somewhat fragile.

During the inletting and shaping of the stock, wood has been removed using cutters, rasps, and files. Each of these tools has not only torn away wood at the surface, it has also compressed the individual cell walls well below the surface. Sanding, alone, will not remove these torn fibers or relieve the stresses on the compressed cell walls. We can do both through a process called *whiskering*.

Whiskering, or raising the grain, uses steam to expand the compressed fibers back to their original shape and forces any torn fibers on the surface to stand up so that they can be easily removed. Any torn fibers or areas of compressed wood not removed or relieved prior to the application of the stock finish will eventually show as bumps, unexplained checkerboard patterns, or dark streaks under the final finish of the stock.

Several methods are commonly used to whisker stocks. Each method varies in its effectiveness in raising the torn fibers on the surface and in relieving the compression marks below the surface of the wood. The first method is to lightly dampen the stock with a wet rag and then use a heat source such as the kitchen stove or a heat gun to quickly evaporate the water and thus raise the grain. This method is very effective at causing the torn fibers on the surface to stand up, but unless excessive water is used and allowed to penetrate the wood to the depth of the compressed fibers, this method will often miss areas of compression that will later show up under the completed finish. (NOTE: Although using propane torches as the heat source has been widely written up and suggested, it is entirely too easy to burn or scorch the wood when using this concentrated heat source. Therefore, their use is not recommended unless used with extreme caution, and only then if used with a "spreader tip" on the end of the torch to fan out the flame.)

The second, and more effective method of raising the grain and expanding the compressed fibers, is to use a steam iron and damp cloth to whisker the stock. The cloth is placed on the stock and the iron is applied to the cloth forcing the resulting steam into the stock.

Although care must be used not to "ding" the stock with the iron, this method not only raises the grain on the surface, but also expands any compressed areas below the surface of the wood back to their original shape.

Once the grain has been raised, sandpaper is used to shear the whiskers from the surface of the wood. Although steel wool often has been recommended for this task, its use has several drawbacks. First, the steel wool not only pulls the loose fibers from the surface, it also pulls fibers out from the edge of the pores causing these pores to look larger than they really are. In addition, small pieces of steel wool may break off of the pad and embed themselves into the surface of the wood. Once embedded, these strands of metal are almost impossible to remove and often show through under the completed finish.

The stock should be whiskered between each change of sandpaper grits. Once is generally enough between the very coarse grits like 150 and 220 grit, but it is best to whisker the stock two or three times at the 280 grit sanding, and until the grain stops raising (again two or three times) at the 320 grit level. In any case, the stock must be completely whiskered before any fill coats of stock finish are applied to the stock. Raising the grain after the pores of the wood are filled will force some of the filler out of the pores, only to be sanded down level with the surface of the wood. At a later date this filler will then settle back into the pores, leaving a pitted surface that will look like it was never filled in the first place.

Proper sanding requires a regimented technique. Sand the entire stock with one grade of paper, raise the grain, and then resand the stock with the next finer grade of paper. Start sanding at the same place each time. Never have more than one grade of paper on the bench at any one time. You will eventually grab the wrong grit and have to resand an entire area because you are using a piece of 220 grit paper to sand an area previously sanded with 320 grit. Keep your sandpaper clean by placing each new grit on a fresh piece of newspaper on the bench or you will contaminate the new paper with previous sanding debris and coarser grits than you are using. Never, never, never, drop a piece of paper on the bench or the floor and then pick it up and reuse it, or you will find deep mysterious scratches in the surface as a result.

Lastly, remember that no matter how closely you have inletted the metal into the wood, or how much care you have put into shaping the architectural features of the stock, the entire stocking job can be ruined by careless sanding. Deep scratches under the finish, rounded edges that should have been sharp, or bumps and dips in surfaces that should have been flat are simply not acceptable in a finished stock. Good sanding is not hard to achieve. It only requires careful workmanship, attention to detail, and a little extra time to do correctly. The rewards will be a stock, and a finish, of which you can be proud.

Figures 3-2 through 3-5 show the line flow diagrams of a typical bolt action stock. Sand in the direction indicated by these line flows.

Sanding and Stock Finishing

Figure 3-2

Figure 3-3

Figure 3-4

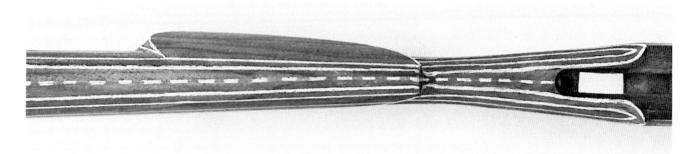

Figure 3-5

Sanding the Right Side of the Buttstock
Figures 3-6 through 3-10

With the stock held by the forearm or barrel in a padded vise, and supported by the third leg, we are ready to start sanding. A good working height seems to be about waist high or slightly higher. With the stock at this height, it is close enough to see the detail of the line and architecture of the stock without having to physically stoop over for long periods, which is tiring and hard on the back. This height also positions the stock so that the stockmaker's forearms travel parallel to the floor for better in-line control of the sanding block.

In general, a wooden block backed with a piece of felt is used during rough sanding to establish and maintain flat surfaces and straight lines over longer distances. For shorter distances, or for the finish sanding where less wood is being removed, a hard felt pad can be used in place of the block.

Both hands are used to control the sanding block. The rear hand provides downward pressure and forward movement, while the front hand provides both downward pressure and rotates the block around the curvature of the stock. Sand with the grain and try to maintain an even pressure across the face of the block.

Only a small portion of the block is in contact with the surface of the wood at any time and a small buildup of sanding dust forms on either side of this area of contact. By watching both the scratches left by the paper and the trail of sanding dust, you can see the exact direction in which you are sanding. Also, the sanding strokes should be of constant velocity and travel the full length of the line flow. Short stroking sands over one area more than the adjacent areas and will result in inducing curvatures and dips into areas that should be flat.

SANDING AND STOCK FINISHING

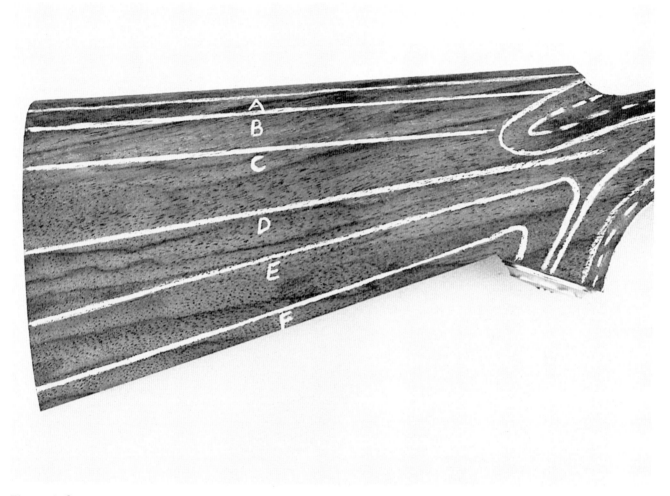

Figure 3-6

In Figure 3-6, the sides of the buttstock are straight tapers that follow the line flow shown. A straightedge placed along any of the flow lines should reveal a flat surface free of any dips or bumps.

Figure 3-7

In Figure 3-7 a wooden block backed with a felt pad is used to rough sand the right side of the butt from line F to the top of the comb line. The rigidity of this pad helps to maintain the straight lines and surfaces of the stock over the longer line flows of the buttstock.

SANDING AND STOCK FINISHING

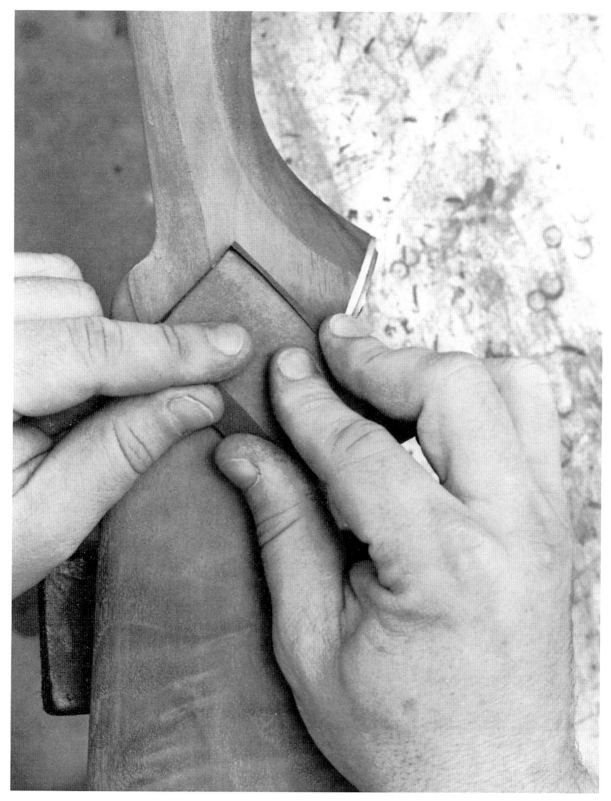

Figure 3-8

In Figure 3-8 the block has been replaced with a hard felt pad to sand line D (Figure 3-6) through the pistol grip.

Figure 3-9

Sanding the Side Profile Line of the Wrist

The side of the wrist curves outward from the center of the grip to just behind the end of the receiver. This area is rough sanded with the wooden block and backer (Figure 3-9) and finish sanded with the hard felt pad shown in Figure 3-10.

Figure 3-10

Figure 3-10. The hard felt pad provides enough support to sand surfaces smoothly, yet is flexible enough to conform with the shapes or contour being sanded.

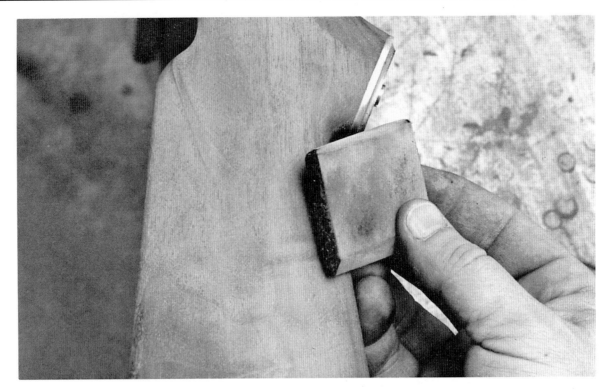

Figure 3-11

Sanding the Lower Right Side of the Butt and the Lower Rear Portion of the Grip

Figures 3-11 and 3-12

To sand these areas we use a hard felt pad with a radius ground on one side as shown in Figure 3-11. As you sand forward, the radius of the pad will climb up the side of the grip and sand it smooth. Rotate the pad as necessary to sand the entire area and feather the rear of the stroke into the area sanded with the block to avoid any overlap or joint lines.

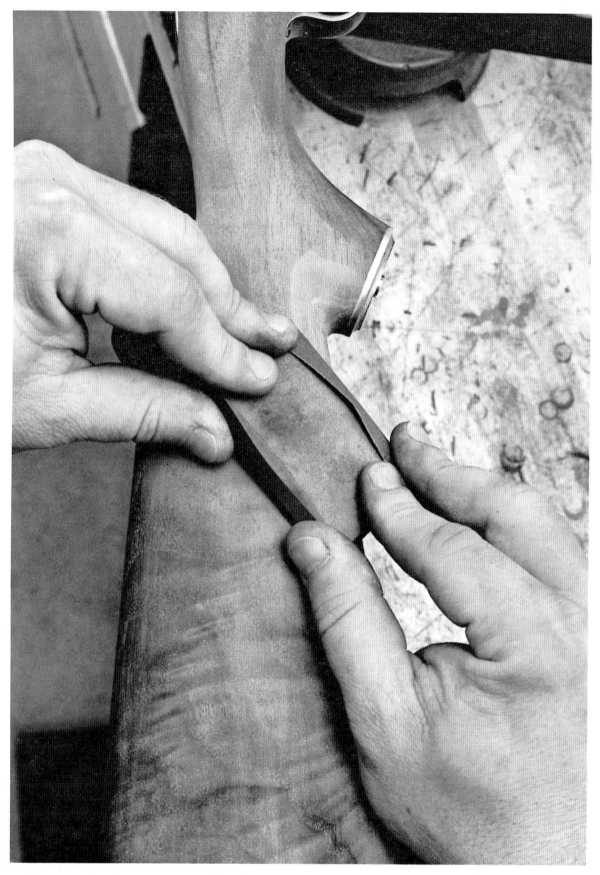

Figure 3-12

Sanding the Toe-Line and the Small Radius at the Rear of the Grip
Figures 3-13 through 3-15

The toe-line of the stock is sanded along the flow lines shown in Figure 3-13.

Note that the cross-section of the toe of the stock, between Lines F on the right and left sides, forms a "V" shape slightly rounded at the bottom, whereas the cross-section directly behind the grip is more rounded into an inverted "U" shape. If this area was laid flat on a piece of paper, it would be readily apparent that the surface area at the toe of the stock is less than the surface area directly behind the grip. Now, if this area is sanded using normal sanding technique (i.e., full-length strokes at a constant pressure), a slight dipping at the toe will occur because you are removing more wood from the smaller surface area. To counteract this dipping effect and sand this area correctly, simply exert less downward pressure on the pad when sanding over the toe than when sanding up toward the rear of the grip. Although varying the pressure on the pad would normally induce a dip in the area of greater pressure, the fact that when using full-length sanding strokes you are sanding over the surface area of the toe more often, tends to offset this slight dipping effect and you end up with flat, straight lines.

NOTE: Some things are easier to demonstrate than to put into words. If the above discussion doesn't make a lot of sense to you, try sanding this area with a constant pressure on the block first, and then try varying the pressure along the length of the stroke. The result may surprise you, especially if you use a straightedge to check on the flatness of the lines.

SANDING AND STOCK FINISHING

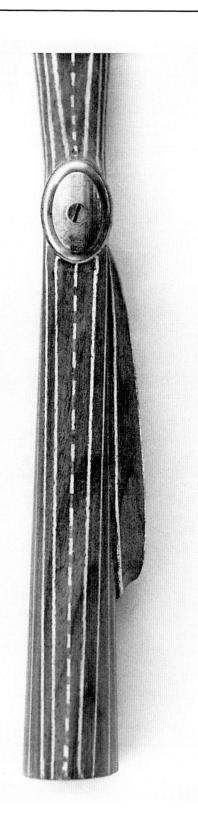

Figure 3-13

Figure 3-13 Line flow diagram of the toe-line of the buttstock. Note that the lines on either side of the dotted center line form an area that is wider at the grip than at the toe.

Figure 3-14

The toe-line of the buttstock is rough sanded with the wooden block to establish and maintain its straight lines and finish sanded with the hard felt pad as shown in Figure 3-14.

In Figure 3-15, the small radius between the grip and the toe-line is being sanded. Use a small mandrel, such as a dowel rod or drill bit to roll a tube of sandpaper several layers thick and slightly smaller than the radius being sanded. Place this tube at the beginning of the radius and rotate your wrists and hands upward. Repeat this motion until the entire radius is sanded.

SANDING AND STOCK FINISHING

Figure 3-15

Figure 3-16

Sanding the Lower Left Side of the Buttstock and Grip
Figures 3-16 through 3-19

The left side of the buttstock is sanded along the flow lines shown in Figure 3-16. A straightedge placed along any of these lines should reveal a perfectly flat (level) surface. Note that both lines D and E extend into the pistol-grip of the stock.

Figure 3-17

As shown in Figure 3-17, a flat steel bar is used to rough-sand the area between lines E and F directly beneath the cheekpiece. The hard felt pad will be used later for the finish sanding of this area. This is a difficult area to sand properly and you should check the line flow frequently for any bumps or dips of the surface.

Figure 3-18

Figures 3-18 and 3-19 illustrate the sanding technique used to sand the lower rear side of the grip. On the right-hand side we were able to sand from the rear forward and let the radius of the pad ride up into this area to sand it. On the left side, however, the cheekpiece sticks out too far to get the proper angle. To sand this area we must sand backward with the radiused edge of the

Figure 3-19

hard felt pad. Position the pad at the top edge of the line flow and draw it back toward you as shown in Figures 3-18 and 3-19. Rotate it slightly and draw it back again until all of this area is sanded. Stop just as the radius of the pad contacts the straight side of the stock.

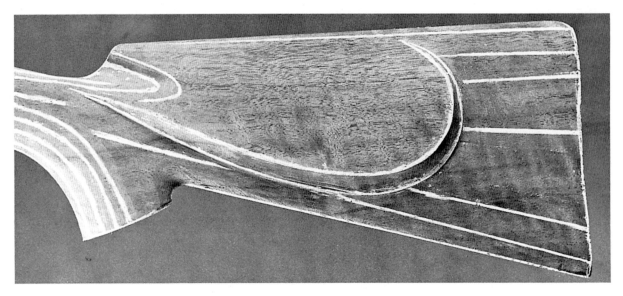

Figure 3-20

Sanding Behind and Below the Cheekpiece
Figures 3-20 through 3-28

The left side of the buttstock involves the most intricate sanding on the stock. The simple straight line flows of the right side of the butt are interrupted on the left side by the cheekpiece. The line flows are the same on both sides of the stock, however, and we do have the right side to look at and study.

Although there are various sizes and shapes of cheekpieces used on modern sporter stocks, they basically fall into two categories — ghosted or unghosted. The sanding of a ghost-line cheekpiece is illustrated here. The sanding of the unghosted cheekpiece is discussed at the end of this section.

A ghost-lined cheekpiece is delineated by a small shelf of wood on its lower edge of the side bevel. This shelf complicates the sanding in that we must figure out how to smoothly sand all the way to the shelf without any bumps or dips in the surface. To further complicate the issue, the outlining of the cheekpiece makes it a separate entity from the rest of the buttstock and any line flow or taper that is not perfectly symmetrical with the corresponding line on the right side of the buttstock will stand out like a sore thumb.

The cheekpiece side of the stock is rough sanded using a flat, steel

Figure 3-21   Figure 3-22

bar as the backer for the sandpaper. Follow the flow lines in Figure 3-20. The sanding movement is straight ahead from the back of the stock to the edge of the cheekpiece. The square edge of the bar, combined with its rigidity, allows us to sand right up to this edge as illustrated in Figures 3-21 and 3-22.

Figure 3-23

As you sand, rotate the leading edge of the bar slightly and walk the sanding lines around the side curvature of the butt as illustrated in Figures 3-23 and 3-24. Pay particular attention to the area directly behind the upper rear of the cheekpiece. This is a hard area to sand, and these line flows must be both straight and flat in order to be entirely correct. This is an area where many

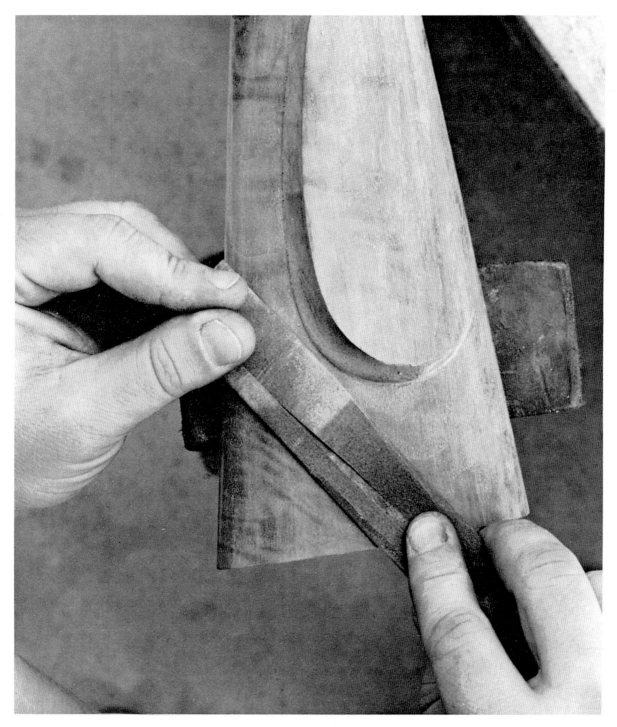

Figure 3-24

stockmakers, even many professionals, fall short. Take your time. Frequently check the surface with a piece of ground die stock or straightedge. It is tedious and slow work, but there are no excuses for dips or bumps behind the cheekpiece.

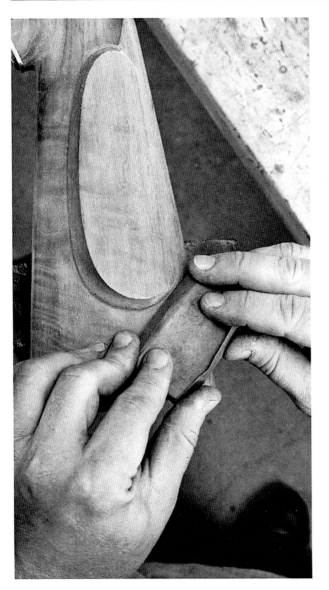

Figure 3-25

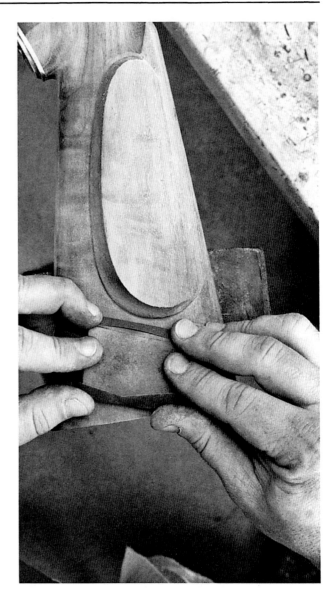

Figure 3-26

Figures 3-25 through 3-28 illustrate the use of the hard felt pad for the finish sanding of these areas. Turn back to Figure 3-11 for a moment. Notice that the hard felt pad has a radius on one end and a bevel on the other end. We sand this area with the bevel side toward the cheekpiece. Once again, the leading edge of the pad is angled slightly as the pad sands along the flow lines. Particular care must be used when sanding the straight line flows directly beneath the cheekpiece in order to maintain and sand these lines straight and flat.

NOTE: Although not illustrated, the hard felt pad, *radiused edge forward*,

Sanding and Stock Finishing

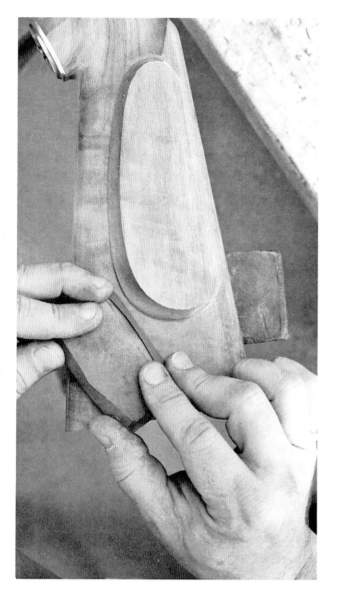

Figure 3-27

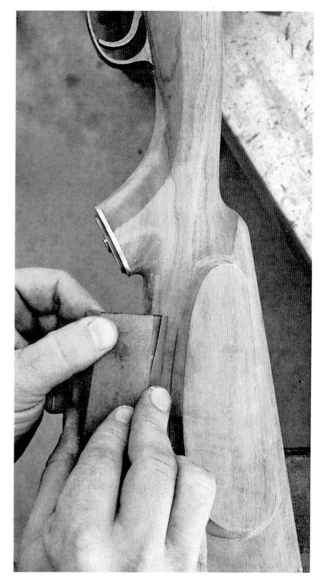

Figure 3-28

is used to sand behind and below the non-ghostlined cheekpiece whose sides are radiused directly into the side of the stock. As you sand along the flow lines, rotate the leading edge (radiused edge) of the pad slightly and allow the radius to slide partway up, and therefore sand, the side radius of the cheekpiece. Radius felt blocks of various sizes, or rubber tubing, are then used to finish the sanding of the side radius of this type of cheekpiece. Stocks with non-ghostline cheekpieces are easier to sand than stocks with a ghostline, as the radius blends into the side of the stock and tends to hide minor errors in the flow or taper from one side of the buttstock to the other.

Figure 3-29

Sanding in Front of the Cheekpiece
Figures 3-29 and 3-30

The small area of wood between the front of the cheekpiece and the center of the wrist is sanded with the hard felt pad, beveled side toward the cheekpiece. The pad is pulled backward along the flow lines, rotated slightly,

Figure 3-30

and then drawn back again until this area is completely sanded.

Any areas that cannot be reached with the hard felt pad can be sanded by wrapping the sandpaper around an emery board for a backer. Be careful, however, that the emery board doesn't cut through the sandpaper and scratch the stock.

Once this area is sanded, continue sanding forward along the left side of the grip and wrist.

Sanding the Cheekpiece

Figures 3-31 through 3-35

Most cheekpieces have flat taper from the back to the front and are slightly curved from the top to the bottom. The wooden sanding block is used to maintain these flat line flows as shown in Figure 3-31.

The radius on the side of the cheekpiece is sanded with a series of shaped backers as shown in Figures 3-32 through 3-35. Thick-walled rubber tubing or cylindrical tubing can also be used as backers, but the author prefers various sizes of felt pads radiused on one edge for this job. The straight sides of the radiused felt pad allows the stockmaker to angle the pad slightly when sanding at the very ends of the cheekpiece radius in order to avoid inadvertently touching the side of the stock with the sandpaper. A layer of masking tape on the side of the stock also helps prevent cross-sanding marks in those areas where the radius and edge of the cheekpiece taper down to nothing at the side of the stock.

NOTE: In order to fit one vertical and four horizontal photographs into the design format of the book, Figure 3-31 (sanding the outer surface of the cheekpiece) was illustrated before the sanding of the side radius. This is technically incorrect. It is a cardinal rule in sanding that when sanding any area that has sharp edges you first sand that portion that may round off the sharp edge then sand the area that will resharpen that edge. In this case, you should sand the side radius of the cheekpiece first, then sand the outer flat, portion.

Other areas of the stock where this rule also applies are the top of the wrist and fluting in the nose of the comb, the finger clearance arch (on the side and to the front of the trigger guard), and the little fillets that form the transition shapes between the forearm and the body of the stock through the receiver area. In fact, in order to reestablish and maintain the sharp edges, it often is helpful to sand the fillets and radiuses one grit or grade of sandpaper finer than that which you are using to sand the flat areas. That is, sand the radiuses with 400 grit paper before you sand the flat surfaces with 320 grit paper. Little tricks like this make the difference between an amateur and a professional sanding job.

SANDING AND STOCK FINISHING

Figure 3-31

Professional Stockmaking

Figure 3-32

Figure 3-33

Sanding and Stock Finishing

Figure 3-34

Figure 3-35

PROFESSIONAL STOCKMAKING

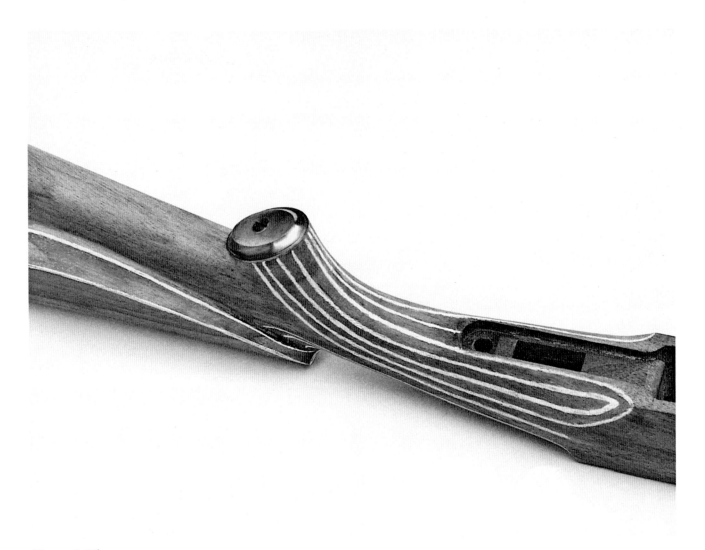

Figure 3-36

Sanding the Front and Lower Sides of the Pistol Grip
Figures 3-36 through 3-40

A medium-hard felt pad is used to sand the front and lower sides of the pistol grip as illustrated in Figures 5-41 through 5-44. The pad is held as shown with the outer fingers pulling up at the edges of the pad while the middle fingers push down in the center to form a shallow "U" shape. This shaping and the medium hardness of the pad allow its surface to closely conform to the curvature of the grip and sand it evenly.

SANDING AND STOCK FINISHING

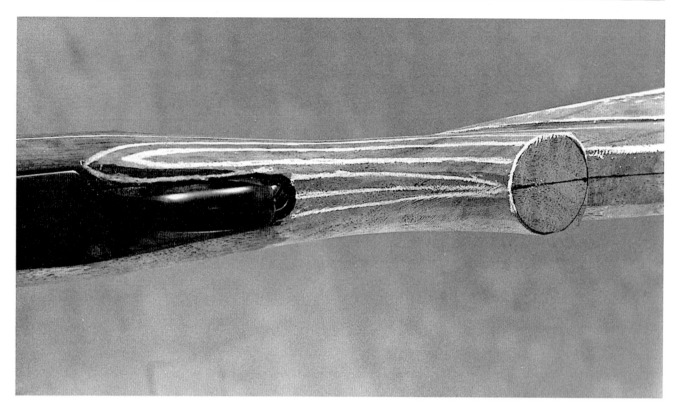

Figure 3-37

Figure 3-38

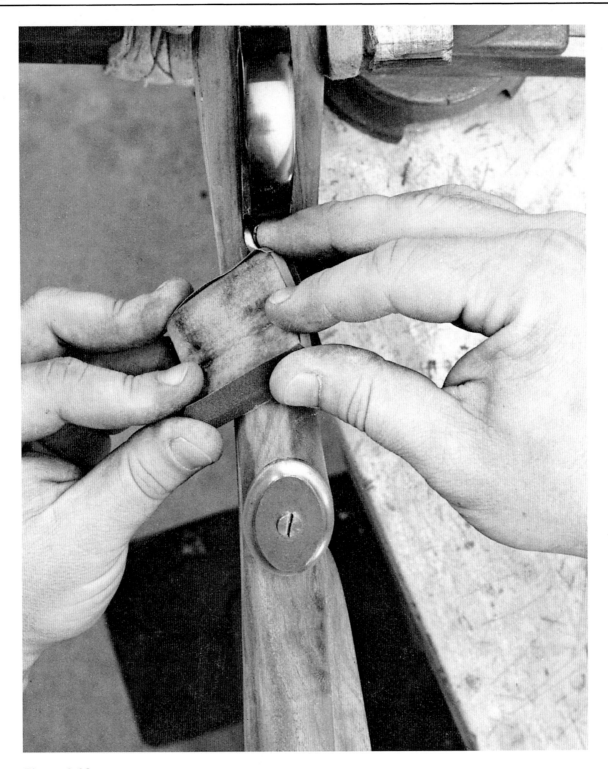

Figure 3-39

NOTE: Although it looks like we are sanding across the grain in these illustrations, we are not. The front of the grip, the nose of the comb, the front and back of the cheekpiece radii, and end of the forearm tip are areas of end grain and as such can be sanded in any direction without leaving cross-grain sanding scratches in the surface.

SANDING AND STOCK FINISHING

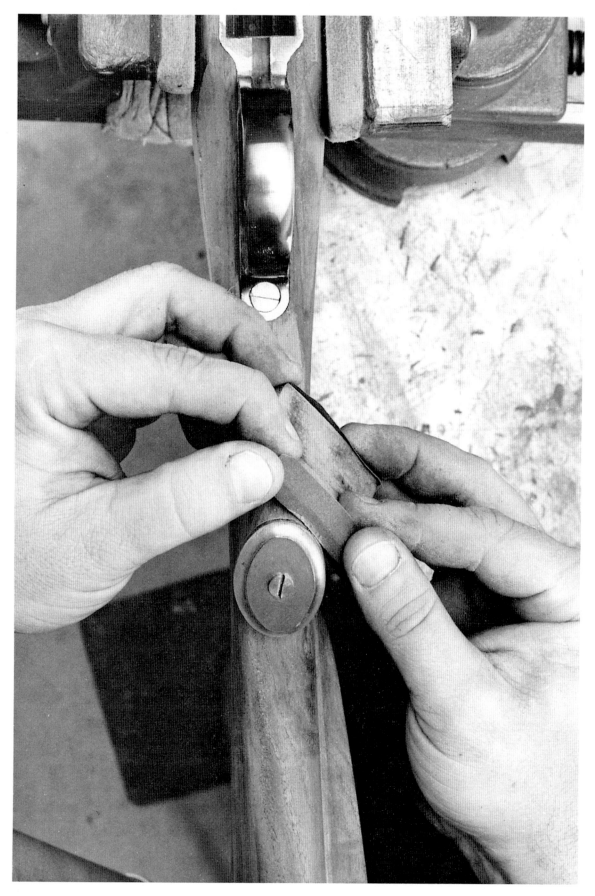

Figure 3-40

PROFESSIONAL STOCKMAKING

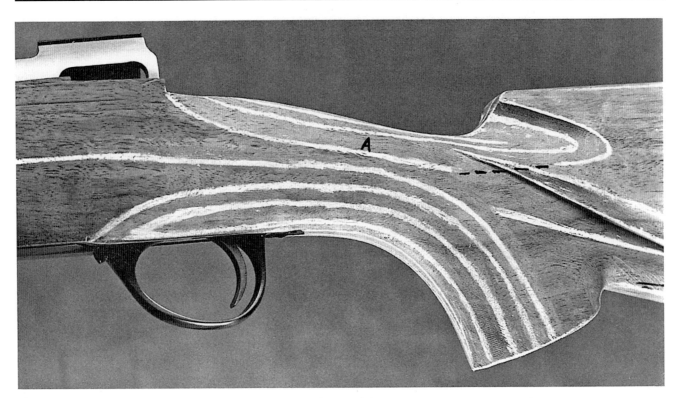

Figure 3-41

Sanding the Finger Clearance Arch
Figures 3-41 through 3-43

This area forms the transition between the lower front of the wrist and the lower body of the stock through the receiver area. Its function is to provide ample clearance for the trigger finger to reach the trigger, hence its name, the *finger clearance arch*. The trigger guard/magazine box is removed while sanding this area so that we can obtain the correct sanding angles with the pad. Sand along the flow lines illustrated in Figure 3-41 and also review Figures 3-36 and 3-37. Rotate the front edge of the hard felt pad as necessary to sand the sides and front curvature of the arch. Feather this area into the sanding lines along the sides and front of the grip.

NOTE: Because the author was either too busy or too lazy to rearrange the lights and move the camera, the stock is shown clamped by the buttstock in Figures 3-42 and 3-43. A better way to hold the stock while sanding this area is to place a dowel rod in the barrel channel to protect the edges of the inletting, and then clamp the stock by the forearm and use the third leg to support the rear of the stock.

Sanding and Stock Finishing

Figure 3-42

Figure 3-43

Professional Stockmaking

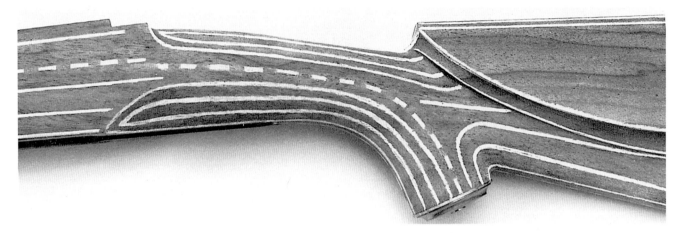

Figure 3-44

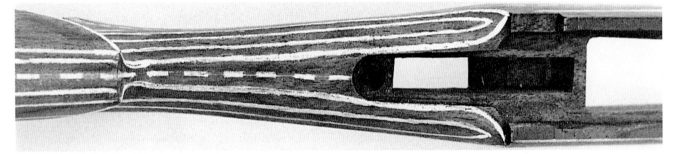

Figure 3-45

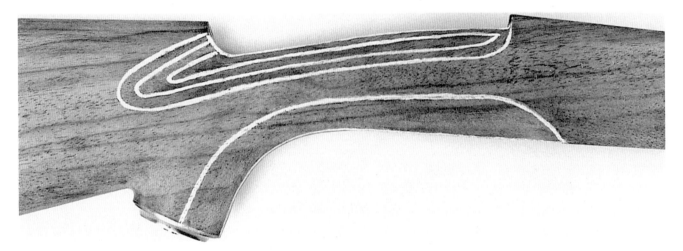

Figure 3-46

Sanding the Upper Wrist and the Comb Nose Fluting
Figures 3-44 through 3-51

Figures 3-44 through 3-46 show the line flows of the wrist. Notice the line that delineates the top of the wrist from the side profile of the stock also forms the bottom line of the fluting in the comb.

Sanding and Stock Finishing

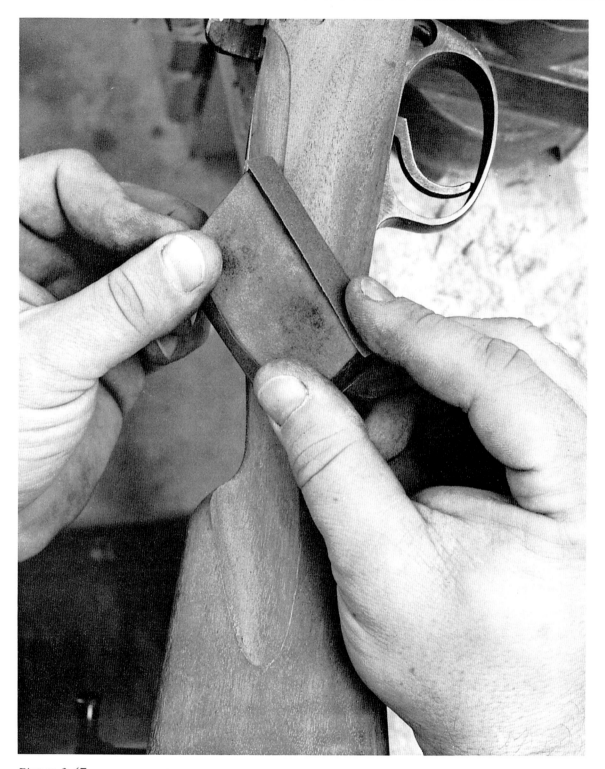

Figure 3-47

Figures 3-47 through 3-51 show the hard felt pad being used to sand these flow lines. Sand from the center of the wrist backward with the radiused edge of the pad facing the flute. As you sand, rotate the pad as shown. The radius of the pad follows the concave shape of the flute and will sand the entire flute evenly, right up to its upper edge.

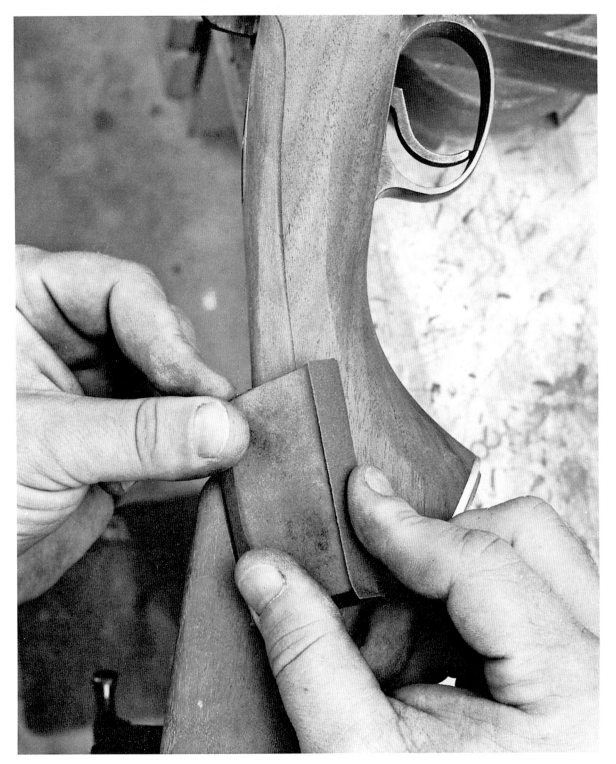

Figure 3-48

NOTE: In regard to Figures 3-48 and 3-49, be careful that the pad doesn't ride up over and round the top edge of the fluting, which should be a sharp line. If this rounding occurs, however, the line can be reestablished by sanding the side of the buttstock down slightly using the wooden block as a backer.

Sanding and Stock Finishing

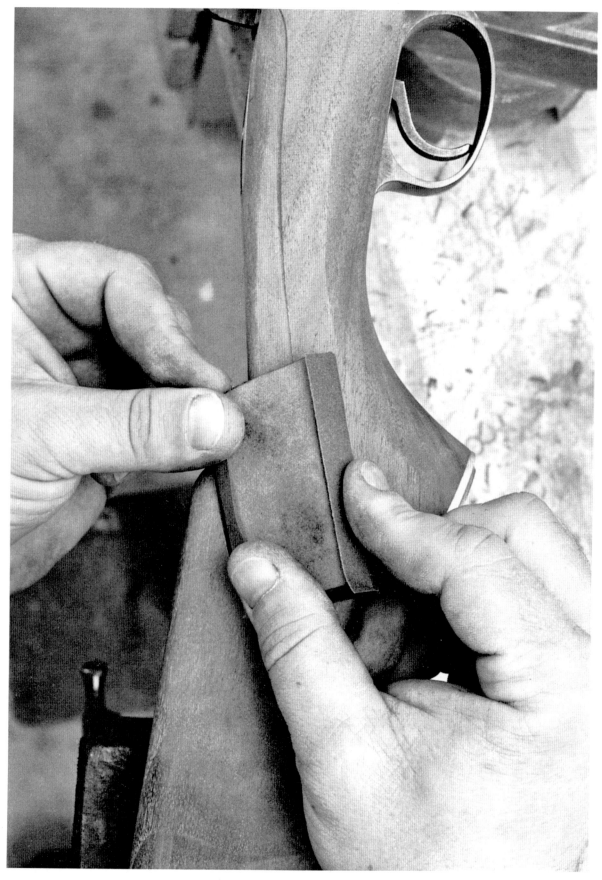

Figure 3-49

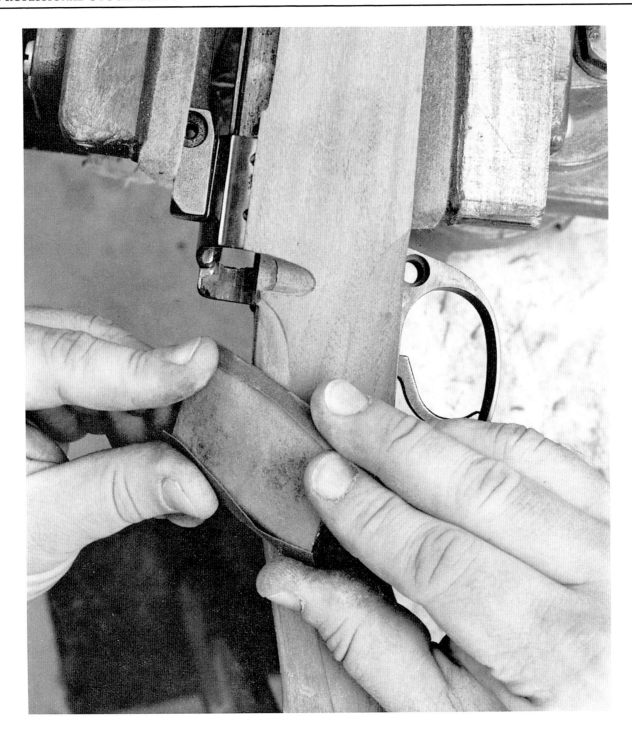

Figure 3-50

The top of the wrist is sanded along the flow lines in Figures 3-45 and 3-46. Reverse the hard felt pad so that the radiused edge is to the front. Sand from the middle of the wrist forward allowing the radius of the pad to slide onto, and thus sand, the fillets which form the transition between the wrist and the body of the stock. Start sanding at approximately the middle of wrist and feather these sanding lines into those formed in Figures 3-47 and 3-49.

Sanding and Stock Finishing

Figure 3-51

PROFESSIONAL STOCKMAKING

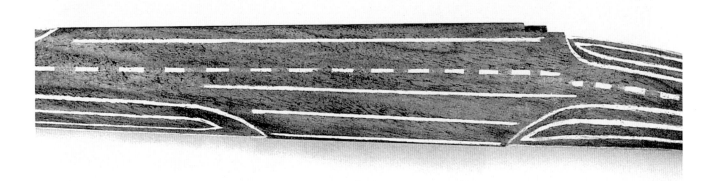

Figure 3-52

Sanding the Body of the Stock Through the Receiver Area
Figures 3-52 and 3-53

The body of the stock is sanded along the flow lines shown in Figure 3-52. The stock can have two basic profiles through this section: the first, a straight taper from the rear of the receiver to the forearm tip; or, second, a straight taper from the rear of the receiver to the front of the receiver, followed by another taper from the front of the receiver to the forearm tip.

In either case, note that the flow lines above and below the side profiling line extend out into the forearm, and should be sanded accordingly. The wooden block is used in order to maintain a true and level surface throughout.

Do not cut the ejection port at this stage. The wood in the port serves as a bridge for sanding and helps to maintain the straight line flow in this area.

Sanding and Stock Finishing

Figure 3-53

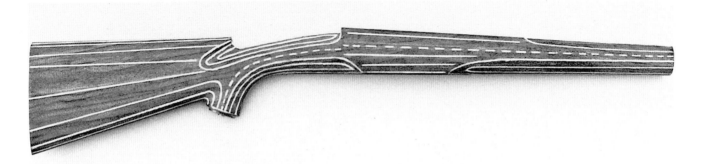

Figure 3-54

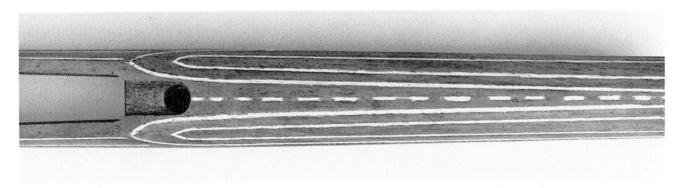

Figure 3-55

Sanding the Forearm
Figures 3-54 through 3-57

The sides and bottom of the forearm have some of the longest, straight, flat line flows of the entire stock. Sand the forearm from the tip backward toward the action/trigger guard using the wooden block for all but those little fillets on the sides of the front tang of the magazine box and on the top of the forearm next to the barrel. Use the radiused felt pad in those areas and blend it back into the area sanded with the block. Rotate the stock slightly after every couple of passes so that the area being sanded is uppermost for better control in sanding the line flow in this area.

Because of the length of the forearm, it is very easy to sand dips or leave bumps in areas that should be flat. Check for this by squinting down the stock from front to back. Any bumps and dips in the surface are readily apparent and can be smoothed out with either sandpaper or by draw-filing. Try to keep both sides of the stock symmetric throughout. It is easily enough done, it just takes patience.

SANDING AND STOCK FINISHING

Figure 3-56

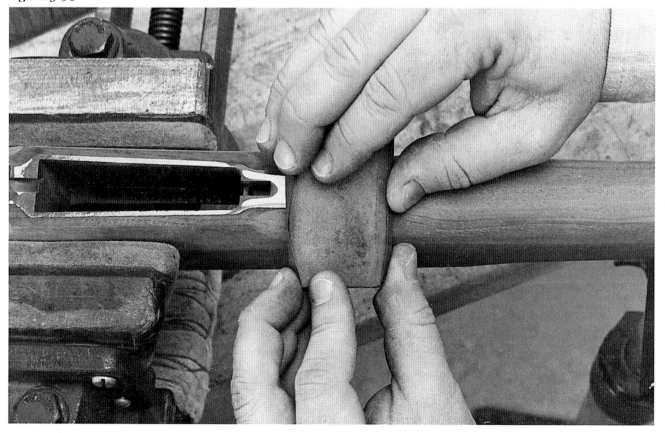

Figure 3-57

SANDING AND STOCK FINISHING
Part 2 - Stock Finishing
Section 1 - Introduction

The function of the finish of a gunstock is to protect the surface of the wood from mild abrasions and wear, to provide a barrier against moisture from entering or leaving the woods, and to enhance and show the grain and figure of the wood to its best advantage. Each of these functions will be discussed in turn.

Concerning the first function, protecting the stock from abrasions, there are two schools of thought. The first school says that a "built-up" finish that coats the surface of the wood with several layers of finish protects the wood better than an "in-the-wood" finish that exposes the surface of the wood to direct contact with any abrasive agents. Both schools have their pluses and minuses. Whereas it is true that a buildup of finish on the surface of the wood *may* prevent minor scratches from damaging the wood itself, it is also true that trying to repair or spot refinish a "built-up" finish, without the underlying layers of finish showing, can be next to impossible. On the other hand, minor abrasions or scratches on an "in-the-wood" finish can be easily repaired by sanding out the damaged area and rubbing in several new coats of finish.

The second function of the finish is to provide a moisture barrier for the wood of the stock. Although to some degree both the built-up and in-the-wood finishes protect the stock from absorbing moisture, *no* finish will completely seal the stock from absorbing moisture from the atmosphere, nor should any attempt be made to do so.

Wood is a dynamic entity. Throughout its life, first as a tree and then as a stock, the wood has continually expanded and contracted from the absorption or loss of moisture.

During the 1960s several major U.S. arms companies began using an epoxy finish on their guns. While this finish was truly impervious to moisture, it was not impervious to atmospheric moisture. Look at those same stocks today, 30 years later, and you will see that the stocks that had relatively straight grain, which is prone to less movement, still have a good finish on them. However, on those stocks made from highly figured and unstable wood, the finish has been cracked in a checkerboard pattern from the movement of the wood due to the absorption and release of moisture from the atmosphere. As long as the stock finish prevents the gross absorbing of moisture (rain or snow), the inherent tendency of the stock to move or warp is dependent solely on the stability and grain structure of the individual stock. If a particular stock is going to warp, it will do so no matter what finish is used. Granted, you may be able to slow down the movement but you will not be able to stop it by attempting to completely seal the stock. In fact, trying to completely seal the stock, as in the case of glass bedding the inletting, may actually induce stock warpage by not allowing the wood to absorb moisture evenly throughout.

The third function of the stock finish, the enhancement of the grain structure and figure in the wood, is purely aesthetic and a judgment call on the part of the individual stockmaker. To the author's eye, no other finish even comes close to the beauty of the traditional hand rubbed oil finish. But beauty is in the eye of the beholder, and if you prefer appearance of the high, gloss built-up finish, then by all means, that is the finish you should use.

SANDING AND STOCK FINISHING

Section 2 — Stock Finishing

Several years ago, after a particularly long day talking to people at the Dallas Safari Club convention, the author had the pleasure of being invited to dinner with master stockmakers Dale Goens and Greg Boeke. During the course of the evening, as often happens when two or more stockmakers get together, the subject of conversation turned to stock finishes. We talked for several hours, or perhaps more correctly, they talked and I avidly listened to what they had to say. Having never found a finish that I was completely satisfied with, I had hoped that one of them had found a secret formula that would fill the pores with one coat, could be used either as an in-the-wood or built-up finish, dried quickly, and rubbed out easily to any desired sheen. To my chagrin I learned that neither Dale nor Greg had, up to that time, found what they considered to be the perfect finish. They, like myself, had not only tried many of the old-time formulas, but were also testing almost every new product that came on the market. To be perfectly fair to the commercial finishes available, however, I must admit that all three of us agreed that the same finish, applied with slightly different techniques by two different stock-makers, could yield vastly different results. Perhaps that is the secret. Perhaps the perfect formula, using my finishing techniques, will someday give me the perfect finish. I haven't found it yet, but I fully intend to continue looking and testing. Who knows, it may be the next one that I try. I doubt it, but it is always good to dream. [Author's note: After having written the above paragraph I decided to give Dale a call. At age 77, with over 38 years in the stockmaking trade, he is still looking. He is currently testing a biodegradable furniture finish out of Europe. Oh well.]

Bearing in mind that different finishes and finishing techniques produce different results for each individual stockmaker, and in order to present as many finishes and techniques as possible to the reader, the author has asked several of the most respected people in the trade to write down their thoughts and techniques on finishing. The author is, and the reader should be, indebted to these men for freely giving both their time and their knowledge. First, however, the author will describe several of the finishes and finishing techniques that he uses.

The first finish, the hand-rubbed linseed oil finish, is a perfectionist's finish. Although the technique for using this finish is quite simple and straightforward, the total time it takes to complete and the amount of labor involved is such that I only use this finish on the highest-grade wood. (From start to finish, no pun intended, this finish can take up to 6 months to complete.)

The procedure is as follows. First sand the stock down to 400 grit paper, whiskering between grits until the grain stops rising. Then use compressed air, followed by a thorough washing down with mineral spirits and a soft bristled brush to completely remove all sanding dust from the pores of the wood and traces of oil from the surface of the stock. (At this point I remove the gripcap and buttplate, or pad, from the stock. These must be replaced after the initial coats of finish have been applied and prior to any further sanding of the stock.) In a clean can mix 1 cup of boiled linseed oil, a couple of tablespoons of turpentine, and 1/2- to 1-teaspoon of Japan drier. Place this mixture on a hotplate (low heat) and heat until it is very warm to the touch but not hot enough to smoke. Remove the can and turn the hotplate up to high. Hold the stock 18 to 24 inches above the hotplate and warm all areas of the stock evenly. (The stock should just be warm to the touch *not* hot.) Next, using a fine bristled brush, slop the linseed oil mixture over the entire stock. Continue brushing the oil mixture onto the stock until the stock refuses to absorb more oil. (Pay particular attention to the wood under the gripcap and buttplate as these areas are "end grain" and will soak up a lot of oil.) Set the stock aside for an hour or so. Any areas where the oil has completely soaked in should be recoated with *warm* oil at this time. Set the stock aside for another hour and then thoroughly wipe any excess oil from all surfaces of the stock. Wait another hour or so and again check and re-wipe the stock. (Author's note: Immediately dispose of all paper towels or rags that have linseed oil on them in an *outside* trash can. Under the right conditions these rags can spontaneously ignite in a matter of 2 or 3 hours and burn the shop down.) Set the stock in a warm, dry place for 8 to 10 days to allow this base coat of oil to dry. NOTE: We have thinned and warmed the oil and warmed the wood of the stock in an effort to force this base coat of oil as deeply as possible into the wood. Although we have added Japan drier to the oil to help speed up the drying time, 8 to 10 days drying time is mandatory even if you live in a dry climate or use a drying cabinet. If you live in a damp or cold climate 2 to 3 weeks drying time is not excessive for this first coat of oil. The biggest mistake made in using a linseed oil finish is to apply the next coat of oil before the previous coat has had time to thoroughly dry. The second biggest mistake is to leave oil to dry on the surface of the stock. This creates a gummy mess that must be sanded off before any further coats of finish can be applied.

After the initial base coat has been given enough time to dry, the next step in the finishing process is the "sealing" of the wood. For this I use a product called Birchwood Casey True Oil Finish, thinned with lacquer thinner. Apply this mixture with a small brush and thoroughly soak the entire stock, paying special attention to the wood under the grip cap and buttplate. This is a penetrating coat and any residual oil on the surface should be wiped off. Set the stock aside for a couple of days to dry and then replace the buttplate and grip cap onto the stock.

After a couple of days drying time brush on one more coat of the thinner/True Oil mixture onto the stock and into the inletting. With the exception of a good coat of paste wax at the very end of the finishing process, this second coating of thinned True Oil completes the finishing of the inletting. Any additional finish slopped into the inletting from here on out should be immediately wiped off.

The next step is to fill the pores of the wood. For this step I use two or three coats of *straight* True Oil applied with my fingers. Allow at least two days drying time between coats. Carefully examine the stock after each coating and use a Q-tip™ to remove any runs or pooling of the finish around the edges of the cheekpiece. Set the stock aside for five or six days to allow the oil to cure and harden completely.

After the initial "fill coats" have cured, use 500-grit wet or dry automotive paper to dry-sand the stock back down to the surface of the wood. Most or all of the pores in the wood should be at least partially, if not completely, filled at this point. Examine the surface of the stock. Pores that are completely filled will be dull in appearance. Any pores that are not completely filled will be shiny and another fill coat or two of finish must be applied and the stock sanded back down to bare wood again.

Now the fun begins. Now the true work involved in a hand-rubbed oil finish starts. Wet the palm of your hand with straight boiled linseed oil and begin to rub it into the stock. You should use enough pressure so the friction of rubbing in the oil causes the surface of the wood and your palm to get uncomfortably warm. (The calluses that you built up on your hands during the inletting, shaping, and sanding of the stock will be worn completely off by the time you have completed your first oil finish.) Rub the oil in until the stock feels *dry*, and then thoroughly wipe the stock with a paper towel. (It is important that *no* oil be left to dry on the surface of the wood.) Set the stock aside to dry for at least six or seven days. Repeat the above procedure and rub an additional 2 coats of oil into the stock.

After the third coat of oil has been rubbed in and allowed to dry, wet sand the stock with 600-grit wet or dry automotive paper using the linseed oil as a wetting agent. (Any spots where oil was previously left to dry on the surface will become readily apparent as the sandpaper will clog and gum up in those areas.) After the stock has been wet sanded with 600-grit paper, rub the stock down with your hand until it feels dry. Set the stock aside to dry.

Rub in several additional coats of oil and then wet sand the stock with 1000-grit wet or dry paper. Rub in an additional 2 or 3 coats of oil and finish the sanding with 1200-grit wet or dry paper. Continue to rub in the oil and wet sand the stock with 1200-grit paper until the wood quits absorbing oil and a single drop of oil is sufficient to coat the entire stock. At that point, and only at that point, is the finish complete. Set the stock aside to dry for a couple of weeks and then give the entire stock a good coating of paste furniture wax.

In the author's opinion, no other finish can match the beauty of a hand-rubbed linseed oil finish. Whereas it is the most time consuming and labor-intensive finish, and although it is one of the least effective finishes in terms of being a moisture barrier (the wax helps a lot), it is easily repairable and the only finish the author considers appropriate for use on exhibition grade wood.

The second finishing technique the author will describe is a "build-up" type finish using Birchwood Casey True Oil for both the pore filling operation and the final build-up finish on the surface of the stock. This technique proceeds in exactly the same manner as the hand-rubbed linseed oil finish through the 500-grit sanding of the pore-filling stages.

After the pores of the wood have been filled and the stock dry sanded back to bare wood with the 500-grit paper, I begin to apply the build-up coats of finish to the surface of the stock with a cloth dobber. (To make the dobber use a 4-inch square of cloth from an old lint-free tee-shirt. In the center of the square place three or four cotton balls and then fold over the edges of the cloth to make the completed dobber resemble an old-fashioned powder puff. A rubber band is used to hold the edges of the cloth in place. Note that these dobbers are not reusable and a new dobber must be made for each additional coat of finish.) To transfer the True Oil from the bottle to the dobber, simply place the smooth side of the dobber against the mouth of the bottle and invert both. The cotton balls on the inside act as a reservoir for the oil, so it isn't necessary nor desirable to leave excessive oil on the cloth face of the dobber. (The secret to a good built-up finish is to apply many very thin coats of finish as opposed to one or two heavy coats.)

Hold the stock by placing one hand through the magazine box inletting mortice and use long strokes to carefully wipe a thin coat of finish onto the outside of the stock. Any runs or puddling of the finish around the edges of the cheekpiece must be immediately wiped off as the thickness of the oil in a run will prevent the finish from drying or hardening properly. Set the stock aside in the drying cabinet, or other warm, dust-free place, to dry for a couple of days. Wipe on an additional 2 or 3 coats, allowing sufficient time for the finish to thoroughly dry between coats.

Next, *lightly* dry sand the surface

of the finish with 500-grit wet or dry automotive paper. Sand only enough to remove the "shine" and any minor imperfection or dust motes from the surface. *Do not* sand back to bare wood. (If you do break through the finish, you may as well cut back the entire surface to bare wood as any such areas will likely show through the completed finish.) Apply an additional 3 or 4 coats of finish and then lightly dry sand the stock with 600-grit wet or dry paper. Repeat the above coatings and sandings until the finish is the desired depth, 6 or 7 additional coats, or until you get thoroughly tired of this entire process. After the last coating, set the stock aside for a week or two to allow the finish to cure and completely harden and then again lightly sand the entire stock with 600-grit paper.

At this point in the finish the stockmaker must decide if he wants a high-gloss finish or a softer egg shell satin finish on the stock. If a high-gloss finish is desired, polish the surface with rottenstone and a soft cloth. If the softer, satin finish is desired, simply rub a coat or two of boiled linseed oil onto the lightly sanded (600 grit) stock and the finish is complete, and the stock ready to checker.

Well, that's about all this author can offer the reader on his finishing techniques. At this time I would like to turn you over to several other stockmakers/gunmakers whose work I greatly admire. These men are all "Masters of the Craft." I leave you in good hands.

Stock Finishing

by Monte Mandarino

This description of my finishing technique will assume that the reader already understands the subtleties and nuances of shaping and sanding, and that the stock is perfectly sanded to a 400-grit finish. "Whiskering" or "raising the grain" is the next step that must be taken to avoid the inevitable roughness that occurs if this step is omitted and the stock becomes wet. This process also serves as a kind of stress reliever for the surface, raising any compressed wood that the trauma of shaping may have produced (i.e., rasp marks, small dents, etc.).

Dampen the stock with a well-soaked soft cloth and allow the stock to air-dry for about 30 minutes. Sand whiskers off with 400-grit wet or dry paper and repeat until no more whiskers raise when the stock is dampened, usually four to six times.

The stock is now soaked, inside and out, with a good quality polyurethane finish. (I use John Bivins Express Oil Sealer available from Ted Nicklas, 5504 Hegel Road, Goodrich, Michigan 48438.) The sealer is flowed on with a one-inch wide paint brush on all surfaces including under buttplates and grip caps.

The first coat should be allowed to dry for twenty-four hours to make certain there is a good, dry base to build the finish upon. The next coat is applied with a soft cloth, being careful to not allow the finish to puddle around the shadow line of the cheekpiece behind the pistol grip or other areas that will be difficult to sand blobs of hardened plastic away from. One or two or more coats are applied in this manner until the sealer begins to stand on the surface and dry with a shine rather than soaking into the stock.

You will notice that each subsequent coat dries a bit faster, with the third or fourth coat taking only an hour or two to harden up. It is not necessary nor desirable to add any more sealer to the inlets as they are now as waterproof as they are ever going to be and any more sealer might prevent the metal parts from seating properly into their respective spots.

The stock is now ready to be filled, and for this purpose I prefer making a paste. Three parts powder rottenstone, one part powdered bone black and enough Express Oil Sealer to make a very thick paste seems to do the job for me. I mix the slop up in very small quantities in an old dish on my bench, probably no more than a teaspoonful at one time. The method of application is the real trick here. Stretching a piece of cotton tee-shirt material across my index finger, I dip it into the paste and rub it into the stock surface in a circular motion with a lot of pressure, forcing the paste into the pores. Rub until the surface is almost dry and there is no paste actually on the surface of the stock. Repeat this procedure until the pores are level full, usually three or four times, giving the paste plenty of time to dry between applications, eight to ten hours should do it.

Now, backing your 600-grit wet or dry sandpaper with the proper shaped blocks and using it dampened with plenty of water, cut all of the sealer and filler standing on the surface of the stock back down to bare wood. Concentrate on areas no larger than three or four square inches at a time and keep plenty of paper toweling at hand to dry the excess water and sanding dust from the stock so you can check your progress. You can tell when you have succeeded in getting back down to bare wood because the surface will look bleached when the water evaporates.

It is very important to remove all traces of finish from the stock or the stain we are going to put into the wood will not be evenly absorbed.

"What?" you say, "Stain this $500 piece of Turkish walnut? You must be kidding."

Staining is probably too strong a term for how I color wood. Toning would probably be closer to the method I use, or even warming might be more accurate.

My biggest complaint about much of the modern stock work I see is that the color of the wood is very cold. There is no other way to describe the feeling I am left with when I examine a piece of work that is technically beyond criticism, but just doesn't inspire that warm feeling inside me that truly great work does. Many times I am not even aware of what is wrong until much later when I realize that everything was right except that all important ingredient, color. Humans are very visually oriented and color evokes feeling in every one of us. Just ask a cosmetics specialist or anyone involved with display advertising and they will tell you color influences people. Of course, some blanks need it more than others, but I have yet to make a stock that couldn't benefit from just a little help.

The product I use for this is an alcohol-soluble aniline dye, produced by the J. Behlen Bros. Co. and sold by Wood Finishers Supply, 1267 Mary Drive, Rochester, New York 14502. This stuff comes in powdered form and the two colors I use are walnut and Bismark brown. The powder is very concentrated and I begin by making a dilute solution with solvent alcohol. Experiment on a leftover scrap of wood from making the stock, and make certain that the scrap is sanded just as carefully as the stock to ensure its taking the stain the same way. I prefer a color that is yellowish orange with a bit of red, but personal taste is always the best guide.

Always make the stain less concentrated than you think it should be, as it is much easier to add more to the stock than it is to get it back out once it is too dark. Bear in mind that the color you see when the stock is wet with stain is the color it will be when the final finish is on.

After allowing the stock to thoroughly dry, which shouldn't take you more than an hour or so, you are ready to begin the final finish. My personal preference for a final finish is good old GB linseed oil, available in most gun shops and gunsmith supply houses. I've tried a great many oils, varnishes and polyurethanes but always seem to come back to this old standby. Its slow drying time gives me plenty of time to rub it out until almost dry to the touch, resulting in very little left on the surface and a classic oil finish appearance.

I begin the final finish by saturating the stock liberally with the oil, giving it about 15 minutes to soak in and then wiping off the excess with paper towels until the stock appears dry. Twenty-four hours drying time is essential for this oil as any less prolongs the drying time of each subsequent coat. Two more coats applied in this manner and then the stock is ready for the hand-rubbed treatment.

I dab on a couple of very small "spots" of oil on a four- to six-inch area of stock and rub the surface with the palm of my hand until the stock feels almost dry and then move to the next area. Extreme care must be taken to not leave excess finish on the stock or it will take on a brassy shine that must be cut back with rottenstone.

As with just about every other process in the "Art and Mystery" of gunmaking, you must find your own way. I submit this method as one of many ways to accomplish a satisfactory finish. I hope it is helpful.

Stock Finishing

by Mark Silver

My preference for the look of traditionally stained and finished gunstocks combined with an awareness of the need for more effective functional finishes has led me to look for techniques outside those usually seen in today's stockmaking. A study by the University of Wisconsin Wood Laboratory, published in *Fine Woodworking*, tested the abilities of various wood finishes to significantly slow moisture transfer between the atmosphere and wood samples. Results showed that none of the finishes tested, ranging from linseed oil to various resin varnishes, polyurethanes and epoxies, were effective without a built-up surface film. A well-sealed wood surface made an important contribution to adhesion of the finish but did little to slow atmospheric moisture transfer even though water appeared to "bead" on the surface. Why this emphasis on moisture transfer? Isn't it good enough just to keep the surface from getting wet? As a matter of fact, no. Changes in a stock's moisture content directly affect its dimensional stability, changing pressure on critical areas of barrel and action bedding. Not only is accuracy affected but, perhaps more important, the rifle's ability to retain a consistent point of bullet impact is seriously reduced. This must be the primary consideration in any firearm destined for serious use in the field.

The other major consideration on a fine quality arm is appearance. As in all aspects of fine gun work, function and beauty are not mutually exclusive. Traditionally, most fine guns, whether stocked in European or American walnut, maple or the occasional fruit wood, have been finished by methods that enhanced and deepened their natural colors and markings. Staining, whether produced by a chemical (mordant) or a colored solution (dye), was normally used to achieve various tones of reddish brown with brilliant gold highlights. This is as true of the first part of this century as it is for the sixteenth through the nineteenth centuries. Since the end of World War II, most American custom gunstockers have turned away from the darker-toned, built-up finishes and developed entirely new techniques designed to provide the ultimate surface and edge definition on a perfectly filled, unstained European walnut stock. Their success has produced an impressive visual style of finish, showing high contrast between the light base color and black mineral streaking characteristic of European walnut.

My traditional tastes in gunstocking have led to 12 years of ongoing experimentation aimed at combining the sharp edges and perfectly filled pores of the American Classic style with the darker, richer color tones of traditional British and European stocks. After reading the *Fine Woodworking* article mentioned above, I was forced to add a low-gloss built-up surface film to my list of necessary finish attributes.

Since European walnut is the most appropriate and one of the most difficult stock woods to finish, we'll use it as an example. Wood preparation is the same for either the "in the wood" or built-up finish. After final stock shaping and detailing, sand, using 100-, 150- and 220-grit sandpaper. Whiskering between grit changes assures that all file marks are removed quickly and easily, and that compressed wood fibers don't push through your perfect finish on the first rainy day. Raise the grain or "whiskers" by dampening the stock with a damp cloth and drying rapidly with a propane torch. Always use new sandpaper and light pressure when whiskering to avoid pressing raised fibers back into the wood's surface. Use various shaped sanding blocks with the sandpaper pulled tightly around and creased on the block edges to keep flat surfaces flat, curves well defined, and edges sharp. All inlets should be thoroughly sealed along with the exterior stock surfaces, using a thinner consistency of your stock finish. I use Laurel Mountain Forge Permalyn sealer, a high-quality, exterior-grade oil-modified polyurethane varnish, once marketed as John Bivins' Express Oil. Brushing sealer into the inlets, including under the buttplate and grip-cap areas as well as major barrel, action, magazine bedding recesses, contributes to stock stability and reduces the risk of the wood deteriorating from excess lubricating oil. Two 20-minute sessions, keeping the stock wet by brushing, separated by a full day for drying, seal well. Wipe excess sealer off the surface and out of the inlets after letting the stock absorb all it can for 30 minutes.

Begin the filling process using the higher viscosity Permalyn filler, by rubbing a thin paste mixture of the Permalyn and powdered rottenstone into the pores, then letting the stock dry for 12 hours. Next, wipe on a good coat of plain Permalyn, letting it dry overnight. The rottenstone plays an important part in the later staining process so don't leave it out. Wet sand with 320-grit wet or dry production paper using water as a lubricant. Yes, water! It doesn't penetrate the stock to any extent and it allows us to clearly see that the filler coats are thoroughly cut back to the wood. Any minute amounts of finish left on the surface or in creases, like the cheekpiece shadow line, will cause a blotchy stain job later. At this point, the stock is a hideous washed-out gray mess, but don't panic, it will all turn out fine in the end. Continue the filling by rubbing on a thin coat of rottenstone and finish mixture, followed when dry by two coats of plain Permalyn and wet sanding with 400-grit wet or dry paper and water. Repeat the sequence again, only this time thoroughly wet sand using 600-grit paper and water. The pores should be well filled at this point.

In preparation for staining, wipe the stock down with mineral spirits and let dry for 30 minutes. For best penetration and color, use a solvent-based or NGR stain (non-grain raising); Laurel Mountain Forge's Antique Rifle Stains are excellent. I normally use a mix of 70 to 90% walnut and 10 to 30% cherry (red). Traditional alkanet root dissolved in alcohol could also be used, but it does not give the depth or control of color that the NGR aniline dyes provide. Use the stain full strength unless you only want a light tone; stain jobs invariably tend to lighten as they are finished. Apply the stain with a large swab made of cotton tee-shirt material wound around a 1/4-inch dowel and tied with thread. Use a fairly wet swab with quick strokes, keeping things as even as possible. Don't let any drips or runs dry on the stock. If you plan to stop with an "in the wood" finish, wipe on one thin coat of Permalyn, let dry and then checker as usual (I highly recommend Rene Doiron's carbide tools for cutting the pattern to depth, as normal cutters are quickly dulled by the rottenstone). Yes, the checkering cuts away all the stain. Talk about contrast! Relax. Mix five to eight drops of stain in about 2/3- to 3/4- teaspoon of finish (use an appropriate proportion of walnut and cherry), then, using your finger, dot it around the pattern and brush it

Sanding and Stock Finishing

out with a toothbrush. Wipe an ultra-thin layer of the same mix on the stock surface at the same time and let dry. A second coat on the checkering may be necessary. Monte Mandarino gets the credit for this basic approach to staining and the hideous wet-sanding sequence using water.

Okay, let's back up for a minute. Why mess around with adding rottenstone to the finish during filling? Without it the NGR stain solvents wash filler material out of the pores (using a less tough finish than polyurethane can also cause problems) and leaves you with a less than perfectly filled stock. Why not stain before sealing and filling? The results are uneven and cut away during the wet sanding. How about adding stain to the finish, then filling and wet sanding in the normal way? This results in very little color change and can end in a blotchy job.

The built-up finish just begins at this point. After staining, switch to a quality tung oil/resin varnish adding five to eight drops of stain and coloring the checkering (continuing to use the Permalyn only leads to problems later). Build up thin, even coats of varnish by dotting the finish around an area and then quickly evening it out using the palm of your hand. It is important to work very quickly and evenly, avoiding heavy overlaps between areas. Three to six coats of build up are best, allowing for drying between coats (enough coats for a significant film but not too many to become uneven and lumpy).

After drying for several days, the finish needs to be rubbed out using 4F pumice (using rottenstone in place of pumice produces a very high gloss). On one side of a small saucer or plate put about 1/3-teaspoon of powdered pumice; place a small block under this side of the plate. Then pour a small quantity of "artist's grade" linseed oil on the low side of the plate, keeping the oil and pumice separate. Felt pads (from Brownell's Inc.) in hard and medium grades are used to actually do the rubbing. (Don't try using a cloth or you'll ruin all your work, only the pads provide even pressure and give the control necessary.) Cut several strips 1-inch by 2-1/2-inch from both grades of felt; cutting down onto a soft pine board, use a wide wood chisel to chop them out. Cut one end of a hard felt strip to an angle of about $70°$; again, using the chisel, round off one edge of the other hard pad to use on concave areas like the cheekpiece cove and ejection port ends. Use the medium grade felt for large open areas where you want it to conform to the gentle curves. Dip about 1/2-inch of a strip in the linseed oil, then just barely touch the edge of it into the pumice; it takes very little pumice to do the work. Begin rubbing lightly in a circular pattern; make a few small circles, then using a paper towel, wipe away the oil and pumice to check your progress. Always wipe the pumice off using light, lengthwise strokes. It takes very little rubbing to accomplish this job; remember, we're only trying to even up the surface, not cut through it. Carefully use the cut shapes to get around architectural details on the stock. Always use a light touch, avoid the checkering and don't cut through any edges. This really isn't more difficult than wet sanding, it just takes a little different technique. After a little practice, rubbing out a sporter stock should take about two to two-and-one-half hours. Wipe the stock down with mineral spirits, let dry, then rub on a coat of C.C. Lemon's stock conditioning oil (from Brownells' Inc.).

The built-up finish gives an entirely different look than the "in the wood" types, providing richer colors, great depth and, above all, far more protection for the wood while reducing the possibilities of point-of-impact change due to changes in atmospheric humidity. The higher gloss of this finish tends to magnify any surface finish flaws and make edges look softer than an "in the wood" finish. One possibility worth exploring is the use of varnishes with additives to reduce gloss, the "satin" finishes. Just don't be tempted to use polyurethanes or epoxies in the built-up stage of a finish, these can lead to an uneven appearance due to a visible boundary between layers of finish and poor rub-out properties.

Another highly useful technique is the ability to add black mineral streaking to English walnut. This is particularly useful in restoration work, whether on an eighteenth century Georgian fowler, prewar sporter or a customer's damaged bolt action. When replacing damaged wood by splicing in a new piece, it is never possible to exactly match the existing pattern of mineral streaks in a fine piece of English walnut. The most effective approach is to match the base color, apparent density and grain orientation of the area to be replaced using a plain piece of wood. In other words, match the exact direction and flow of the wood's pores. This is a good bit more tricky and critical than it sounds.

The next step can be done after wet sanding, as outlined above or before any finish is applied, depending on the type of finish to be matched or used. Just remember, any staining, added color, or streaking is strictly on the surface and will be cut away by any abrasive cutting through to the wood's surface. Begin the streaking by drawing a wet Q-tip™ swab along the path you want the streak to follow. Then, using a nib pen (wide nib for wider lines, narrower for thin lines) dipped in black India ink, draw a wet line along the same path. While the ink is still wet, use a dry Q-tip™ to "draw-off" excess water and create the correct type of line to match the original stock. By varying the amount of water used, and technique for drawing off excess water after inking, any type of streaking can be created or matched. This inking takes a bit of experimentation, but is very effective. If you need to erase a line or redo it, just scrub it off with wet then dry Q-tips™ while the ink is still wet.

Stock Finishing

by Ed Webber

Sanded-in finishes have been used by gunmakers in one form or another for years, utilizing a mixture of sanding dust and wood finish to fill the pores in the stock. As with most stock finishes, there is some good news and some bad news concerning the process. The bad news is involved with the fact that sanding in a finish takes time... time spent sanding the stock repeatedly, and time spent waiting for the successive coats of finish to dry. Also, this technique obviously won't work on wood that has to be stained.

The bad news is offset by the ability to obtain a deep, durable, attractive finish that has the advantage of being easily maintained and repaired, and maintenance and repair are real considerations if you are building a rifle that will see much use in the field.

As with any stock finishing technique, the final results are greatly dependent upon the quality and suitability of the materials used. In the never-ending quest for the perfect wood finishing products, the best for this application that I have found so far are Standard Paint Wood-Loc sealer and McCloskey Tungseal tung oil varnish. There probably are equal or better products available, but I haven't stumbled onto them yet.

The first step is to seal the wood inside and out. After the stock has been final sanded with 220-grit paper, remove as much sanding dust as possible with compressed air or a tack rag. It is not necessary to raise the grain before applying the sealer, as any fibers that erupt will be sanded off as the stock is finished. Apply Wood-Loc liberally, going over the wood several times as the finish is absorbed. End grain under the buttplate and in the action mortice will soak up a great deal of Wood-Loc and will continue to draw in the finish for as long as you have the patience to apply it. Once you have applied all the Wood-Loc that you can stand, set the stock aside for at least 24 hours and let the finish cure good and hard. After the stock has dried sufficiently, go over it with Wood-Loc one more time and let it dry for two to three days, depending on temperature and humidity. If a drying cabinet is used, let the stock stand for at least 36 hours. Wood-Loc penetrates relatively deeply, and it takes a bit for the volatile hydrocarbons to evaporate.

After the Wood-Loc is thoroughly dry, wet sand the stock with 320-grit paper, using a 50/50 mix of Wood-Loc and tung oil varnish as the wetting vehicle. Leave the resulting sanding sludge on the wood until it is completely dry. Wet sand this sludge off with 320 paper, wiping the wood surface clean with paper towels as you progress.

At this point, a few comments on sanding are in order. Use sanding blocks to back the sandpaper or you may lose the clean edges and shapes that you are trying to maintain. Sand only enough to achieve a thin "mud" on the stock surface. When removing the dried wood dust/stock finish "mud," sand only enough to remove the surface gunk. Sand too deeply and you will re-open the pores.

Single shot and double gun stocks should have lockplates, receiver, tangs, and buttplates installed to insure that the wood surface remains flush with the metal. Don't use a sanded-in finish on these types of actions if you are trying to save original metal finish, bluing and case colors do not respond well to abrasives. It is better to choose a wood finishing method that doesn't jeopardize the metal finish.

Repeat the wet-sanding process with 400-grit paper and then with 600-grit. This should leave you with a stock that has the pores completely filled. Note: It is important that the finish dries completely between sandings. If each succeeding coat is not absolutely dry, the stock is very apt to develop an orange peel appearing surface a few weeks after it is completed due to the finish in the wood pores drying and shrinking.

If there are still some pores that are not completely filled after the last 600-grit sanding, go over the offending areas once more with the 600-grit paper. This is rarely necessary, and usually only with very open grained wood.

The wood surface should now be ready for the top finish. I have been using straight McCloskey tung oil varnish. It is durable, dries hard, and is easy to work with. The trick in using it lies in applying several very thin coats. Try dabbing five or six drops on approximately a five-inch square area of the buttstock and rubbing it out thinly and evenly with the heel of your hand. Trial and error will quickly give you a feel for how much tung oil varnish is needed for a given area. Rubbed in thin coats will quickly build up to a hard, high-gloss finish. This may be left as is or cut back with rottenstone and rubbed out to a semi-gloss surface. To achieve the appearance of a traditional linseed oil finish, cut the surface back with rottenstone or 0000 steel wool, and hand rub linseed oil in for a final coat. At this point, your patience and perseverance should be rewarded with a stock finish that is both durable and attractive. An occasional application of tung oil varnish to worn areas will keep the stock looking respectable.

Wood-Loc is available from Standard Paint, 3015 Dormax S.W., Grandville, MI 49418. Their phone number is 616-534-3701. Ask for product number 5015.

McCloskey Tungseal tung oil varnish, product number 931, is generally available at most hardware and paint stores. Buy the half-pint tins, as it tends to gel after it has been opened unless you put it in a squeeze bottle and keep the air away from it. Both Wood-Loc and Tungseal can be colored with alkanet root or transparent mineral spirit base stains if you wish to enhance the color of the wood.

Stock Finishing

by Richard Schreiber

Much has been written about the difference in appearance between one stock finish system and another. For years I have heard of the beauty of a hand-rubbed "London Oil" finish on a fine English shotgun, and how plastic modern-day varnishes look. Most of this is personal prejudice and not supported by fact. The only real difference between these two finishes is the surface gloss and the film durability. A varnish can be made to look like a drying oil finish with the proper application methods.

The modern furniture business has started to use a new technology to finish their products. They use a 100% solid resin system, cured by exposure to UV light. The system has advantages in that there are no solvent emissions and the resin cures almost instantly on exposure to UV radiation. However, this finish system has one serious drawback — appearance. UV resins are notorious for curing with a very high gloss, wet-look surface. Great for some uses, but not for fine furniture. It was always easy to pick out pieces finished with UV systems because of the high gloss, but not any more. The technology has advanced to the point that the gloss can be controlled and the quality of the finish is equal to that of any hand-rubbed application. The same is true of stock finishes, with the proper application technique almost any quality finish can be made to give you the appearance you desire.

When selecting the finishing system for a stock, it is important to determine what the ultimate use of the firearm will be and how much time can be spent working on the finish. The finish I may recommend for a stock for someone who only stocks a gun every couple of years may be different than what I may recommend to a professional who finishes the carving on a Friday night and needs to stain and finish the gun for delivery to a customer on Monday morning. The finish for a showpiece firearm may be different than one meant for the day-to-day rigors of a hunting rifle.

There are a great variety of finishes available to the stocker, from the traditional drying oils to modern varnishes. Your choice will depend on a variety of factors.

What are the reasons for applying a finish to wood in the first place? Are you simply trying to preserve the existing beauty of the stock or enhance it? Are you looking for a weatherable coating or just one to keep the dirt off the wood? Are the ease and speed of application important?

The professional stocker usually has a clear idea of what he is trying to achieve. Since time is money, he is always looking for a finishing system that is quick to apply. The durability of the finish is also important as he cannot control the ultimate use of the firearm. With the quality of the finishes available to the stocker today, one should be able to select a finish that
1. Dries fast
2. Enhances the beauty of the wood
3. Is easy to apply
4. Has excellent exterior durability

Due to the advances in modern finish technology, it is easy to obtain these results with a minimum of effort. Even a beginner can achieve professional results the first time by selecting the proper finish and, *most important*, following instructions.

It is important that the stock be whiskered to achieve the best possible finish. Whiskering swells the surface grain of the stock and removes any surface imperfections from the carving process. The surface of the stock has been compressed from the pressure of the various cutters, rasps, files, chisels, and sandpaper used to shape and smooth the wood. Whiskering uses water to swell the surface of the wood, allowing the stocker to use fine sandpaper to remove these imperfections.

To whisker, apply clean water sparingly to the surface of the stock using a clean, lint-free cloth. Apply only enough water to slightly moisten the surface. It is important to keep the amount of water you use to a bare minimum. If you use too much, you stand the risk of getting water too deep into the pores and swelling the stock. This can spoil any inletting you may have done.

I like to work on small areas at a time, about 12 square inches. Though you can let the stock air dry, the use of heat speeds the evaporation rate and helps insure that no residual moisture is left. To apply heat, use an electric heat gun or hair drier. Some stockers will use a propane torch, but this can be difficult to control. If you are not careful it is very easy to char the wood, especially around any sharp edges of the stock.

Application of heat raises the grain much more efficiently than simply allowing the stock to air dry. This technique is especially useful in removing surface dents and compression. Drying the stock quickly limits the depth of moisture penetration into the wood. You only want penetration into the outermost layers of the stock. Deeper penetration can destroy the quality of tight metal inletting and destroy accuracy.

Once the stock is dry, completely resand the surface lightly using a piece of fine sandpaper, 360 grit works well. Be careful at this point, because you should only sand enough to remove the raised wood grain and nothing more. Repeat the process of dampening the stock, drying, and lightly sanding until the grain no longer raises after the application of water.

A technique I like to use on light colored woods is to tint the first coat of water I use for whiskering. I tint the water with a water-soluble brown dye. The type you use is immaterial, even Rit fabric dye will work. By adding dye to the first water coat, you can more readily see any remaining sanding scratches, carving nicks and other surface defects. The stain will color these defects darker than the surrounding wood. The next sanding operation should be thorough enough to remove these defects.

It is usually a good idea not to whisker areas that have checkering or any decorative carving. Any application of water to this area will swell the compressed wood grain fibers and destroy the carving. In these areas, I whisker the area prior to any carving. This will at least remove any gross compression of the wood fibers before you start to carve or checker.

After the last sanding, the stock needs to be carefully examined for any remaining surface defects. I take the stock into a darkened room and train a bright spotlight on the surface. By careful examination of the stock surface, with the light striking the surface at an oblique angle, any surface imperfections can be easily spotted. If necessary, resand and whisker these areas until you are satisfied with the smoothness of the stock. Remember, this will be your last chance to correct any defects in the stock surface. After the finish is applied, the gloss of the finish will magnify any surface irregularities which remain. With all the time you have invested in shaping the stock, the extra time spent in surface preparation is time well spent. There is a natural tendency to rush the completion of the stock at this point. The stocker can see the end of many hours of sweat and labor, and the desire to rush the finishing process can be almost overwhelming. It is at this point that many a fine piece can be ruined by a poorly executed finishing process.

Now that the stock has been carefully examined, it needs to be thoroughly cleaned. I use a soft brush attached to my shop vac, going over every nook and cranny on the stock. Make sure any residual sanding dust is removed from the lock mortice, barrel channel, and from around any carving. If you have an air compressor, use it to blow off the surface as a final cleaning. I do not like to use a tack rag as the stocks I make usually have a lot of detailed carving. I find that it is too easy to snag and damage the wood at this stage, when using a tack rag. In addition, tack rags are not effective in removing sanding dust from incised lines and checkering.

If you are going to stain the stock, you should do a little experimenting at this point. One thing I always do, and recommend to others, is to always prepare sample blocks with the same wood, stain, and finish, which will be used on the stock. By doing this you are not experimenting on the final product. Remember, wood is a living thing with no two pieces behaving exactly alike. By doing this you will never find out too late that the stock needed to be stained or stained differently, or that you had to use a special finishing technique to achieve the effect you wanted.

If you are working with a naturally dark colored hardwood, such as walnut, you may not need or want to stain the stock. Lighter colored woods, such as maple, usually require the application of stain to enhance the figure of the wood and tone down the "whiteness" of the wood.

When selecting a stain, many factors must be considered. Most important, the stain should be lightfast. Many of the "hobbyist" type stains that you can purchase at your local hardware store or lumberyard are meant for interior use on furniture. Since interior stains are really not subjected to the damaging effects of intense UV light, they usually are not formulated with expensive UV-resistant ingredients.

The stain you use should be a non-grain-raising type. I do not recommend the use of water-based stains. If you have any carving or checkering on the stock, the use of water-based stains will severely swell these areas. There is no advantage in using water-based stains, as there are numerous NGR-type systems available to the finisher, which far exceed the durability and quality of water-based systems.

For the best appearance, dye type stains are the best choice. Dye-based stains are transparent, allowing the natural beauty of the stock to show through. Since the stains are actually dissolved in a solvent carrier, they penetrate deeper into the stock. This makes the stain more wear resistant. Any abrasion that removes the finish coat will usually not remove the stain.

Pigment stains are manufactured with ground, opaque ingredients, in an oil or resinous base. By their very nature, pigment stains cloud and hide the wood grain. Because of the relatively large size of the pigment particles, very little penetration of the wood fibers occurs. Minor surface abrasion usually removes these stains, exposing the raw wood below. Another disadvantage of pigment stains is the oil or resinous carrier. These drying oils, or resins, are usually of a lower quality since the manufacturer has assumed there will be no exterior exposure. This stain can degrade the overall performance of the finish you apply over it.

When applying stains, it is always better to use multiple coats. In this manner you can "sneak up" on the color you want. A heavily applied single coat often overshoots the intensity of color you were trying to achieve. It is always easier to build the color up gradually than to make it too dark and have to work it back. Multiple coats of stain also yield better color penetration into the wood.

After application of the stain, follow the manufacturer's recommendation for dry time, prior to application of the finish. It is important that sufficient time be allowed for the carrier solvents to evaporate. If you apply the finish too soon the carrier solvents in the stain can retard the cure of the finish coats and increase your overall time to finish the stock.

Over the past 30 years I have tried almost all the finishes and finishing methods commonly used for wood surfaces. Some methods work better than others when finishing a gunstock. As I mentioned before, the best stock finishes require not only durability but also the beauty of a fine furniture finish. The fact that the stock usually has detailed relief and incised carving also adds to the difficulty. Over the years I have developed a system that I use almost exclusively.

First, the room where you apply the finish should be clean and dry. For best results the temperature should be somewhere between 65 to 75 degrees. Attach a convenient hook to either the butt or forearm, which can be used to hang the stock to dry after the finish is applied.

For maximum durability it is important that the stock be sealed against moisture damage. This means that all surfaces, including the inside of all inletted areas, barrel channel, and under the buttplate, should be coated with a penetrating type sealer. The purpose of this coating is to sink as deeply as possible, into the wood fibers of the stock to insure that any surface wear will not violate the integrity of this moisture barrier. The only finishing system I use is Laurel Mountain Forge's Permalyn Sealer and Permalyn Gun Stock Finish.

To apply Permalyn Sealer, use it as it comes from the can, without further reduction. Using a soft-bristled brush, liberally apply the sealer to all wood surfaces. The idea is to apply as much sealer as the wood will absorb. Suspend the stock by the hook you previously attached. Place newspapers and an old pie tin under the stock to catch the drips of sealer that will run off the stock. Once you have saturated the stock with sealer, allow the stock to sit undisturbed for about 10 minutes. After 10 minutes re-examine the stock carefully, looking for any areas where the sealer may have puddled on the surface. Pay particular attention to the barrel channel, morticed areas, and around any carving or checkering you might have.

You should find that the wood has absorbed all traces of sealer. If you find any areas with sealer still remaining on the surface, carefully remove any excess with a soft, lint-free piece of cloth. If you find any excess sealer in incised carving or checkering, remove this with a soft-bristled brush. I like to use an old worn out toothbrush for this. Because so much sealer has been absorbed by the stock, it is best that this first coat of sealer be allowed to dry overnight before continuing. If time is a critical factor in your finishing process, you can proceed with the next step after allowing the sealer to dry three or four hours, as long as your room temperature is not too cold.

I always apply some of my finish or sealer to a glass plate at the same time I am applying a coat to the stock. Allow the glass plate to remain in the same general area as the stock. When the finish on the plate appears to be dry, you can be sure the finish on the stock is at about the same degree of cure.

When the first coat of sealer is dry, apply a second coat in exactly the same manner as before. The second coat of sealer will probably not penetrate as well as the first. Because of this, it is very important that the visual inspection for excess surface sealer be very thorough. Allow this second coat of sealer to dry for three or four hours, or until the sealer is dry to the touch. Continue applying sealer and allowing it to dry until you first start to notice a slight gloss build up on the stock surface. This is your indication that the sealer has done its job and you are now ready to start applying finish. The number of coats of sealer it takes to get to this point is naturally dependent on the porosity of the wood. For normal density stock woods, only two coats of sealer are required. I usually start finishing a stock on Friday night. I apply one coat of sealer in the evening, allow to dry overnight, then apply another coat Saturday morning.

After the last coat of sealer has dried, you are now ready to apply the finish coats. Permalyn Gun Stock finish was designed to build more rapidly than the sealer. It also has some unique drying properties that allow it to be applied by hand, like an oil finish.

I prefer applying finish in the following manner, as it gives me more control of the application process. The finish is applied straight from the can, without reduction. Apply the finish to a small area of the stock by daubing the finish evenly over the surface. I use my fingers, but a soft lint-free cloth would work just as well. The secret is to apply just the right amount. You are trying to build the finish up in the wood, not pile it up on the surface. If you apply too much the final result will look like the stock is encased in plastic.

Apply the finish to one side of the butt first. Distribute the finish by rubbing lightly with the fleshy part of the palm of your hand. Initially rub briskly, with moderate pressure. At first the finish will feel slippery and oily, but as you continue to rub you will feel the friction warm the stock and the finish start to dry. At this point, begin to relax the pressure until, finally, you are only lightly skimming over the surface. If you were to grab the stock at this point you would be able to mar the surface, so some care is required in handling. If you find you have marred the surface with a fingerprint, palm print, or other type of surface damage, just add some additional finish to the damaged area. The damaged spot will be redissolved, allowing the area to be smoothed again.

Once you get an area covered, move on to an adjacent spot. I prefer to work on one side of the butt, then the other. Next, I finish the comb, wrist, and then finish up with the forearm. Remember, the finish is still tender at this point. Do not touch the surface until the finish has dried more thoroughly. As when applying sealer, applying some finish to a glass plate and placing it near the stock, will give you a good idea of the degree of cure on the stock itself.

After the first coat of finish has dried sufficiently, usually about three hours, apply another coat in the same manner. Repeat this process of applying a coat of finish until you can see the finish start to build up on the surface. The point when this occurs is determined strictly by experience and judgment. The best indication is when the gloss level starts to build and the small wood pores appear to be filled. The number of coats it takes is dependent on your technique and how porous the wood is. On a maple stock it typically takes only two coats.

Once the finish starts to build on the surface of the stock, it is important that the surface of the stock be smoothed lightly between coats with 0000 steel wool. This serves not only to level the surface and remove any imperfections, but it also enhances the adhesion between coats. After steel wooling the stock, vacuum the surface carefully to remove all traces of the steel wool and the dust from the smoothed finish.

When you apply the first couple of coats of finish it is not usually necessary to roughen the surface. The first couple of coats of finish are still mostly filling the wood grain and do not need to be smoothed by steel wooling.

At this point you need to proceed carefully. It is important that you take care to apply the finish as evenly as possible. The previous coats were mostly used to fill the remaining large-scale wood pores, and you were able to get away with less care in your application techniques. The remaining coats are what the eye will see as the final finish on the stock. The extra care you take at this point will pay off in less effort needed to smooth the cured finish and a generally more pleasing job. Also, be careful that the finish does not build in any of the checkered areas or next to relief carving. Using the same technique you used with the sealer, go over the area with a soft-bristled brush to lightly smooth away any of the buildup. After brushing the area, resmooth the surface with hand rubbing if necessary.

It is also important not to be too aggressive in the use of the steel wool. If you are not careful, you may wind up removing too much finish. You only need to steel wool enough to smooth the finish. Remember, the finish at this stage is still not fully oxidized. It is cured enough to handle and process, but not enough to take hard abuse. However, within 24 hours the finish becomes much more difficult to smooth, so don't wait too long after the three-hour cure time to start smoothing.

As the gloss on the stock starts to build, you will notice it is taking on the appearance of a nice hand-rubbed oil finish...which is exactly what you are applying, except you are not using a drying oil. When you hand apply a finish in this manner, whether it is an oil or varnish base, you very lightly roughen the surface as your hand slides over the surface. This gives the surface of the stock that soft luster that we all love so much.

Once you have filled all the grain on the stock and you are satisfied with the overall appearance, you need only apply the final smoothing coat. This coat fills the remaining surface scratches and gives you the final gloss. For the final coat I like to use Permalyn Sealer, since it dries a little slower and does not build as fast as the Permalyn Finish.

If you have been happy with the gloss you have been getting prior to steel wooling, continue in the same manner, applying a smooth coat of sealer by hand rubbing. Since you have already built the finish to the desired level, you are only trying to fill the remaining surface imperfections from the steel wooling operation and adjust the final gloss. Permalyn Sealer and Permalyn Finish are made from the same polymer base, so by using sealer as the final coat you will not lower the overall durability of the finish.

If you want a higher gloss, apply the last coat with a lint-free cloth pad. Since you are not roughening the surface, the gloss will be quite high. Make sure you apply this coat with care, as the tendency is to apply too much with a cloth applicator. Remember, since this is the final coat, the pad *must* be totally lint free. Any lint that comes off the pad, will remain in the finish.

Those of you who have worked with hand-rubbed linseed oil finishes will be familiar with this technique. The application method is almost identical, except that you will not have to wait for days to apply additional coats. If you have never tried this technique, try it on some scrap wood first — even an old piece of pine — to get the technique down. This is especially important if you are trying this with a finish other than Permalyn. Not all finishes can be applied in this manner. First of all, the finish must have some unique drying characteristics. You want it to dry fast enough to obtain a reasonable finishing time, yet as it dries it cannot become too tacky or your hand will stick to the stock. It is better to experiment first.

When applying the finish in this manner, you are able to control build-up very easily. The amount you apply per coat is less than you would be able to apply by brush or spraying. This results in a smoother finish. Remember, you are only trying to apply enough finish to fill all the wood pores, with a minimal surface buildup. The finish should be abrasion resistant enough to withstand heavy field usage without having to resort to a thick coating to achieve it.

The total time it takes to finish a stock, using this method, will naturally be dependent on a number of factors:
1. The species of wood and its porosity.
2. Environmental conditions.
3. Technique of the stock finisher.

Typically, I have found that most people are able to start applying sealer to a stock on Friday evening and have it completed by Sunday night. This does require diligence on the finisher's part. After the first overnight coat of sealer, subsequent coats of sealer or finish need to be applied in three- or four-hour intervals.

All the firearms I produce are finished as if they were to receive a lot of hard use. With the proper finishing materials, this finishing technique requires minimal extra time but insures that the firearm will retain its beauty no matter what the usage.

Stock Finishing

by Bruce Farnam

The finishing of gun stocks has no doubt seen more research and development (R&D) than any other phase of stockmaking. It seems that every stockmaker has attempted to discover the perfect finish — one-step application (all pores filled) and last forever!

The finish on a rifle or shotgun is just like the finish on a fine piece of furniture or an automobile. It must be taken care of periodically if it is to last and provide the protection and appearance desired.

The stock-finishing process that I am about to describe provides me with the following pluses: relative ease of application, durability, and ease of maintenance and repair.

Upon completion of shaping the stock and rough sanding with 120-grit paper, I begin sanding the stock with 220-grit to remove the 120-grit marks. The stock is now wet with a rag containing water, and dried with a heat gun, to raise the grain. The raised grain is cut down with 220-grit paper, and then the stock is wet and dried again. I now sand the stock with 280-grit paper to remove the raised grain. Again wet and dried and sanded with 320-grit paper to remove raised grain. The grain is now raised for the final time (generally not much grain is raised), but not sanded. The application of the actual finish now begins.

The finish is comprised of: 1) pure tung oil, 2) alkanet root stain, 3) Japan drier, 4) 4F rottenstone. I use the alkanet root stain mixed with the tung oil to warm up the color of the wood, not to stain the stock. The alkanet dried roots can be purchased at health food stores in one-pound bags. The stain is made by heating turpentine (six-ounce volume) up to about 120 degrees and then placing the dried roots (four-ounce volume) into the container. The stain from the roots will color the turpentine dark, blood red. I allow this to remain on the stove for about 30 minutes until the liquid volume is reduced to about four ounces. Strain this liquid through some old, nylon pantyhose to remove the pieces of root.

Prior to the application of the finish, I wipe the stock with acetone to remove all traces of sanding dust. (I use acetone because it evaporates quickly.) The following finish mixture is applied liberally for three days, twice a day, and allowed to soak into the wood: two parts tung oil, one part stain, and two parts mineral spirits. The thin mixture will soak deeply into the wood. On the fourth day I brush straight Japan drier, available at most paint stores, into the stock twice a day until the stock has a glossy look, usually three or four days. The Japan drier soaks into the wood and dries the tung oil from the inside out to the surface of the wood.

This, I feel, provides a deep, penetrating finish that seals the wood inside and out against weather extremes.

The next finish mixture will be used from here on out: two parts tung oil, one part stain, and 1/2 part Japan drier.

The entire stock is wet sanded with 320-grit, wet or dry paper and wiped dry with soft paper towels. Using a cotton cleaning patch, 3x3 folded, and the above finish, I mix 4F rottenstone into a thin paste on the surface of the stock. This is rubbed all over the stock in a circular motion and then left to dry.

This is the first step to fill the pores. The reason I use rottenstone to fill the pores is that it does not shrink into the pores with age as wood dust and finish does.

After the rottenstone and finish dries (24 hours), the stock is wet sanded with 400-grit paper. Once again, rottenstone and finish are applied and allowed to dry. Repeat the 400-grit wet sanding and apply rottenstone and finish again, and allow it to dry. 600-grit paper is now used to wet sand the stock.

Now take the stock outside into daylight and look at every pore to insure that they are all filled. If not, go back to 400-grit paper and repeat the rottenstone and finish process until you are happy.

I now wet sand the stock with 1000-grit wet or dry paper (available at auto paint stores) to start polishing the finish, this step helps to eliminate the flat look seen on so many stocks wherever a pore is in the stock.

The finish mixture and rottenstone are again applied to the stock. This application is intended to polish the stock. The mixture is then allowed to set for about 30 minutes. Using soft paper towels, I remove almost 98% of the finish mixture and set the stock aside to dry for 24 hours. I repeat this sequence two more times then checker the stock. After this is complete, I repeat the above process two or three more times until I achieve the "look" that I want to see.

This process provides a finish that is "in" the wood, lightly built up on the surface, and produces a warm, pleasant luster. This finish will withstand almost constant use if taken care of periodically. I provide directions and the finish mixture components (no stain) with each stock I complete.

APPENDIX I
INLETTING A STEEL BUTTPLATE

Figures 1 and 2

A patternmaker's gauge is used to make a template of the inside contour of the buttplate. Position this template so that the highest points on the heel and toe meet the line of pitch and the center of the template is located at the desired length of pull.

The bulk of the wood is removed with a bandsaw and then finished up using a Nicholson #50 pattern maker's rasp and wood files. The end at the butt should be square with the geometric center of the buttstock.

In the case of the stock illustrated, the customer specified a cast-off of 1/4-inch and 3/8-inch of toe-out. Toe-out generally exceeds cast-off by 1/8-inch to 1/4-inch.

These points were located and connected with a pencil line. (This line represents the vertical geomet-

Figure 1

Figure 2

ric center of the buttstock.) Center the buttplate on this line and use a wax pencil or crayon to transfer the outline of the buttplate to the stock.

Use the Nicholson #50 to rough shape the first 3/4-inch or so of the buttstock, leaving the wood 1/8-inch heavy all the way around.

APPENDIX I

Figure 3

Layout of the Curved Sides of the Plate
Figures 3 and 4

Pencil rubbings (tracings) are used as templates for roughing-in the dome and curved sides of the buttplate as shown in Figure 3.

Note that the depth of the crown varies from zero to approximately 3/16-inch, and that the side template is offset accordingly.

Figure 4

The narrow blade straight chisel is used to stab in the outlines in Figure 3 to a depth of approximately 1/16-inch as shown in Figure 4. The outline is then rough inletted using a modified deep-mortice chisel and the hand positions shown in Figures 5 and 6.

APPENDIX I

Figure 5

Inletting the Sides and Dome of the Buttplate

Figures 5 through 8

Figures 5 through 8 show the hand positions used in inletting the dome and sides of the buttplate. Ninety percent of the inletting is done with the deep-mortice chisel, but it must be kept razor sharp in order to smoothly cut end grain.

PROFESSIONAL STOCKMAKING

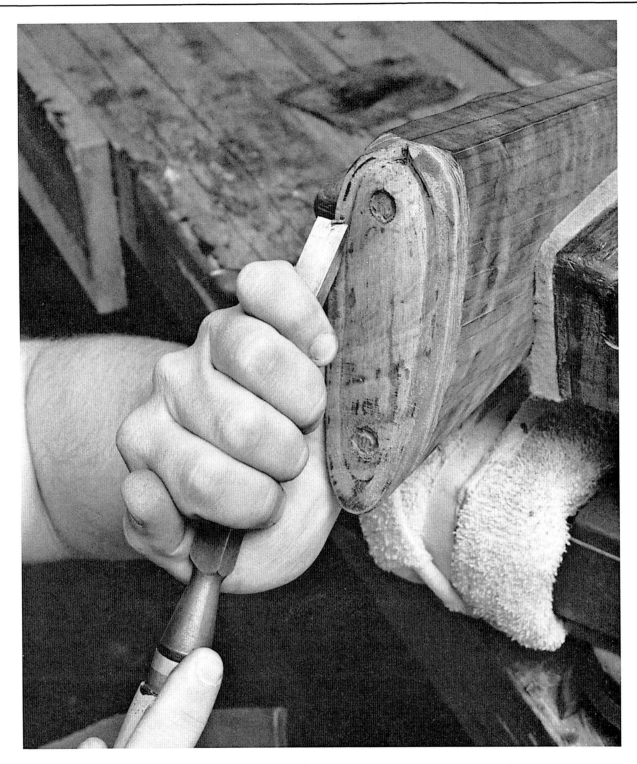

Figure 6

The braced left hand controls the angle of the cutting face of the chisel, and the muscles of the chest and left arm are contracted slightly to provide a rearward resistance to the chisel. The right hand (arm) provides the forward cutting force and steers the chisel through the wood. This is the so-called push-pull muscle control and is necessary for the control of all chisels.

APPENDIX I

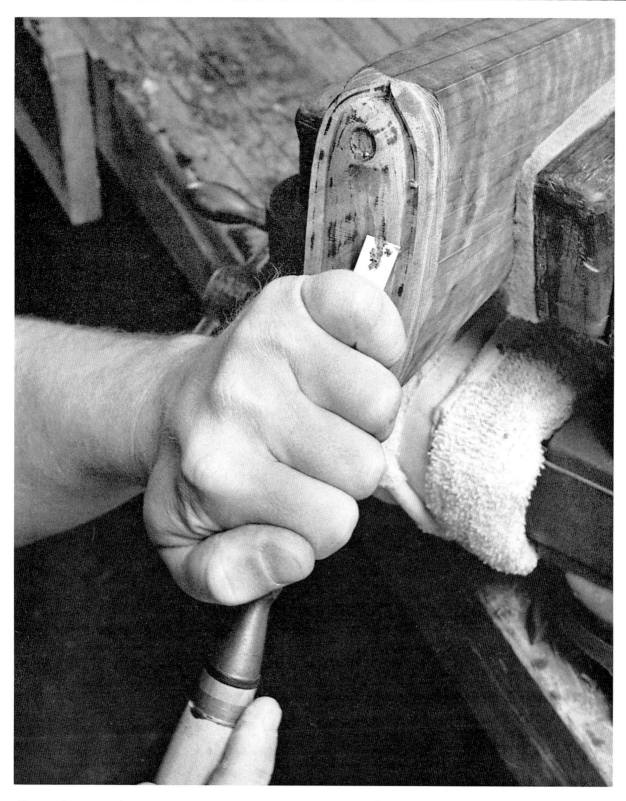

Figure 7

This is one of the few areas in stockmaking when it is easier to work sitting down. The butt of the stock is clamped in the vise and the forearm of the stock rests on the bench to provide additional support to the stock. The work

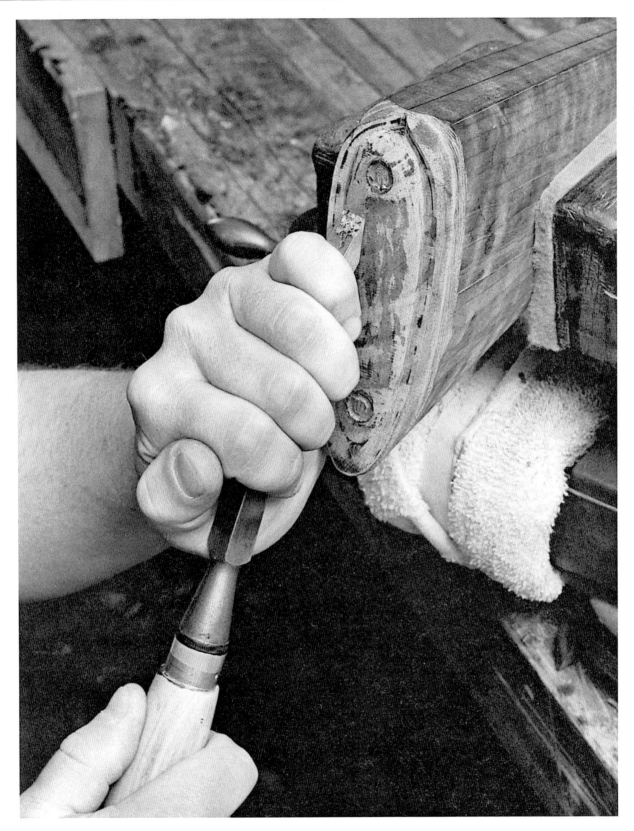

Figure 8

is positioned directly in front of the worker at a height that allows the best leverage and control for these particular cuts.

Appendix I

Figure 9

Cutting in the Tit of the Buttplate
Figure 9

Rough in the dome and align the tit of the plate with the line of the cast-off. Stab in the outline using a small straight chisel. The fingers of the left hand are used to guide and position the chisel in a series of small straight cuts around the curved outside radius of the inletting.

NOTE: Outside radii can be formed by a series of small straight cuts. Go slowly and remove only those areas of contact as shown by the inletting black.

Figure 10

Spotting-In

Figure 10

The accurate transfer of the spotting agent to the wood is critical to good inletting. If the metal shifts, or the coat of inletting black is too heavy, false spotting or contacts will result. Coat the backside of the plate thinly but evenly with inletting black. Position the buttplate as close as possible on the butt and give it one (and only one) light tap with a rawhide mallet.

Patience is the key virtue in inletting. The first couple of "spotting-ins" will show only two or three points of contact. Remove a small shaving of wood at each of these points, recoat, and spot in again. Each successive spotting in will reveal a greater number of contact points that need attention.

APPENDIX I

Use of a Curved Riffler

Figure 11

Wood is a complex vascular system consisting of thick-walled xylem cells and thin-walled phloem cells.

In cutting across the end grain of wood the material is sheared perpendicular to the structure of these cells.

If a stock blank is from a tree that has had a constant rate of growth, the thickness of the cell walls will be uniform throughout, and the chisel will shear them cleanly. If, however, the tree has alternated between periods of fast and slow growth, the cell wall thickness will vary. Such wood will not cut cleanly with constant force.

When wood won't cut smoothly with a chisel, use a curved rasp or riffler to rough shape the inletting.

Because, the greater amount of surface area contacting the wood, the riffler can often be used to smooth out (bridge) the peaks and valleys left by a chisel. The riffler is used only for roughing in. Rasps tear and compress wood, and if used too near the finished edge will leave visible scoring, or compression marks at the juncture of wood and metal. To avoid these marks the final fitting must be done with a chisel or scraper. Note that the edge of the rasp has been ground smooth, or safe, to avoid any unwanted side cuts. The fingers of the left hand are used to guide and position the tool.

Professional Stockmaking

Figure 11

Appendix I

Figure 12

Use of the Flat Scraper
Figures 12 and 13

Figures 12 and 13 show a flat scraper being used to remove the spotting agent from the dome and peripheral flats of the inletting. The left hand steadies the tool and controls the angle of the blade face in relation to the wood.

Figure 13

Scrapers, like chisels, leave an extremely smooth cut and can be used right up to the edge of the wood to metal juncture without fear of leaving compression marks.

Inletting Completed

Figures 14 through 16

The inletting black shows good contact with the dome and, although the edges still need some attention, there are no major gaps along the flat edges. The wood of the dome is flush with the back of the screw holes in the plate. (If the wood is not flush with the back of the plate it is almost impossible to locate the exact centers of the screw holes for drilling.)

The job of locating and drilling these holes can be one of the most frustrating tasks in stockmaking. An off-center screw hole will pull the plate to the side when the screws are inserted and will cause a misalignment of the head of the screw and the countersink in the plate, which in turn shows as a metal to metal gap after the screw head is dressed down. If you drill an off-center screw hole, the only fix is to plug it with a piece of dowel and redrill the hole before proceeding.

Locate and centerpunch the exact center of the screw holes. With the buttplate off the stock, insert the woodscrews into the screw holes in the plate and note the angles at which the screws pass through the plate. The screw holes in the wood must be drilled at these angles. With a crayon or wax pencil, transfer these angles to the stock for use as a guide in drilling.

A hand-cranked "breast drill" is probably the best drill to use for drilling these screw holes. The length of the tool makes it easier to align the angles of the hole, and being hand powered there is less tendency for the drill bit to grab or wander off center.

Align the drill with the wax pencil line on the stock that indicates the correct angle for the screw hole and use a center drill to start the holes. Complete the drilling of the holes using a drill bit that is the same diameter as the screw shank (measured at the bottom of the threads). Too large a hole and the threads will not have enough purchase. Too small and you may well wring off a screw trying to run it home. It only takes one session (usually two to three hours) of try-

Figure 14

ing to dig a broken screw out of a stock before the novice stockmaker understands the importance of using the correct size drill. When each hole has been drilled, remove the bit from the breast drill and re-insert it into each of the screw holes. Check for proper alignment of the drilled holes with the pencil marks on the stock. If the holes are at the correct angle, coat the threads of the screws with beeswax or bar soap and use a properly fitting screwdriver to start them into their respective holes in the butt.

APPENDIX I

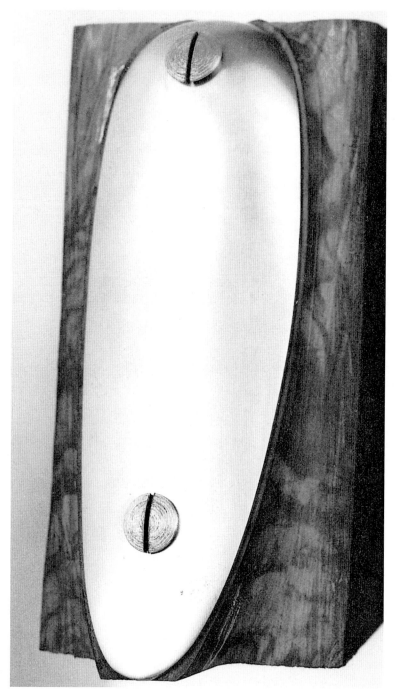

Figure 15

Proceed with the last few spotting-ins. Align the screw slots through the vertical axis of the buttplate, by lapping the countersinks in the plate, undercutting the screw heads, or by inletting the entire buttplate slightly deeper.

Figure 15 illustrates a steel buttplate fit onto a stock being made from the square blank. When stocking from the blank the buttplate is inletted prior to shaping the buttstock.

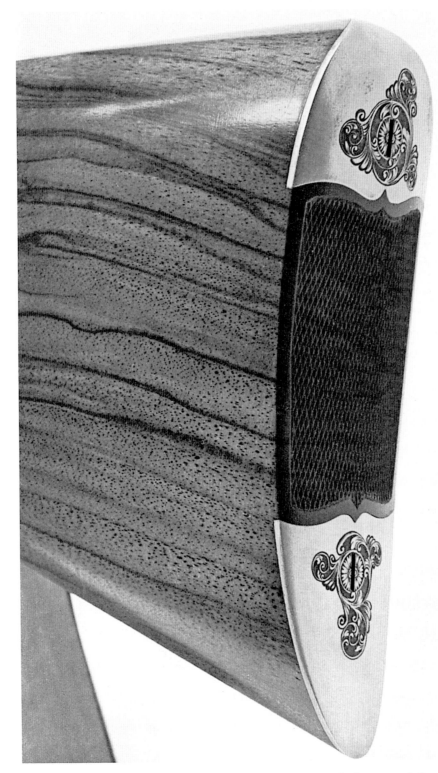

This is an example of a variation of the steel buttplate called a heel-toe clip. Engraving by Jack Haugh

File the heads of the screws flush with the plate and seal the end grain of the stock with finish or with a commercial grain sealer, and the job is done.

APPENDIX I

Skeletonizing Steel Buttplates

Figures 17 through 19

If a rifle is to have a skeleton buttplate, follow the described procedure up through the operation illustrated in Figure 14 (without drilling the screw holes) before skeletonizing the buttplate.

Once the plate has been skeletonized it becomes fragile, subject to easy bending or distortion.

By leaving the plate solid until the operation in Figure 14 is complete, and then skeletonizing it, it is only necessary to inlet the plate an additional depth equal to its thickness and the risk of bending or distorting the plate is minimized.

To lay out the side walls of the skeleton, coat the plate with Dykem transfer dye. Set and lock a pair of dividers (or a hemaphrodite caliper) to a spread of 1/4-inch to 3/8-inch. Use the edge of the plate as a guide for one leg of the caliper and scribe a line in the Dykem on the surface of the plate with the other point of the caliper. The top and bottom of the skeleton can be drawn in freehand or by using the countersinks for the plate screws as a guide. Make the skeleton design symmetrical with the countersinks in the plate.

Figure 17 shows the set up and "V" fixture clamped in place on the bench. Do not try to cut the exact outline at this point, but stay a little inside the lines. Note the extra blades and the piece of beeswax that are kept at hand. The wax is used to lubricate the sawblade as the cut proceeds. These blades are extremely fragile and will break easily so it is best to have several available before starting the operation.

Figure 17

APPENDIX I

Figure 18

In Figure 18, a simple fixture was made from a flat board and dowel rods to hold the plate securely while the skeleton is ground to its final shape.

The grinding stone was reshaped so that it will grind a small bevel (a "draft") along the border of the design. This draft makes the plate easier to inlet without leaving gaps between metal and wood.

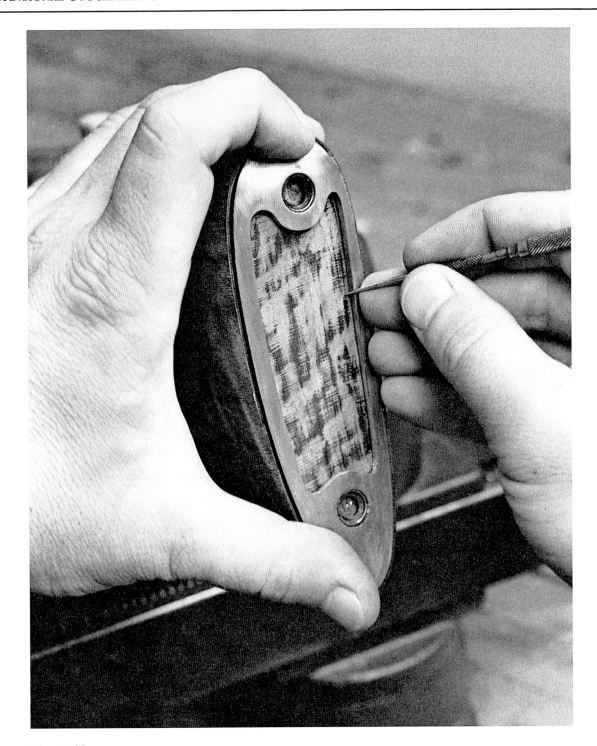

Figure 19

In Figure 19 the skeleton plate is held firmly in position and the outline traced in the wood with a sharp scribe.

Stab in the edges of the outline and inlet to a depth just greater than the thickness of the plate. Insert the screws, dress off the metal and wood together, seal, finish, and checker.

APPENDIX II
TOOLS USED IN STOCKMAKING

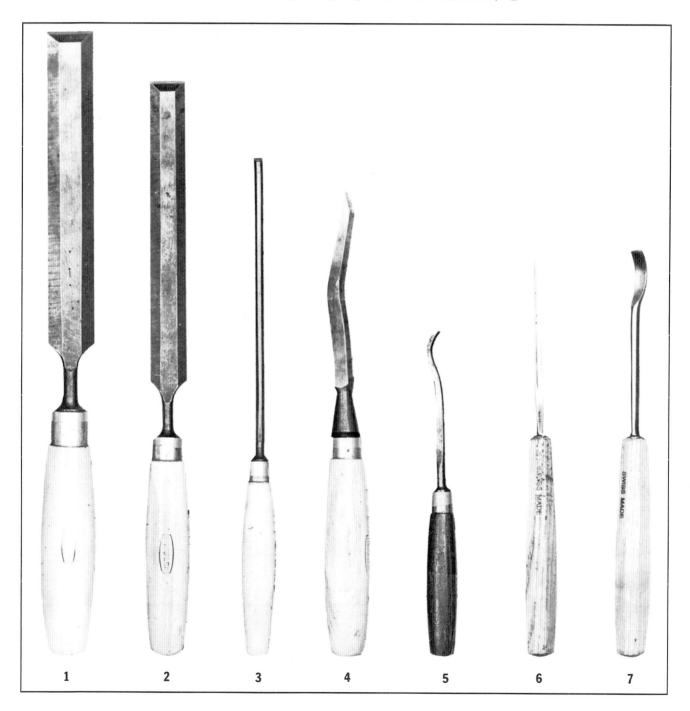

1) 1-1/4-inch paring chisel, 2) 1-inch paring chisel, 3) 1/4-inch paring chisel, 4) 1/2-inch modified deep-mortice chisel, 5) 1/8-inch bottoming chisel, (6) #8-4mm gouge, 7) spoon chisel,

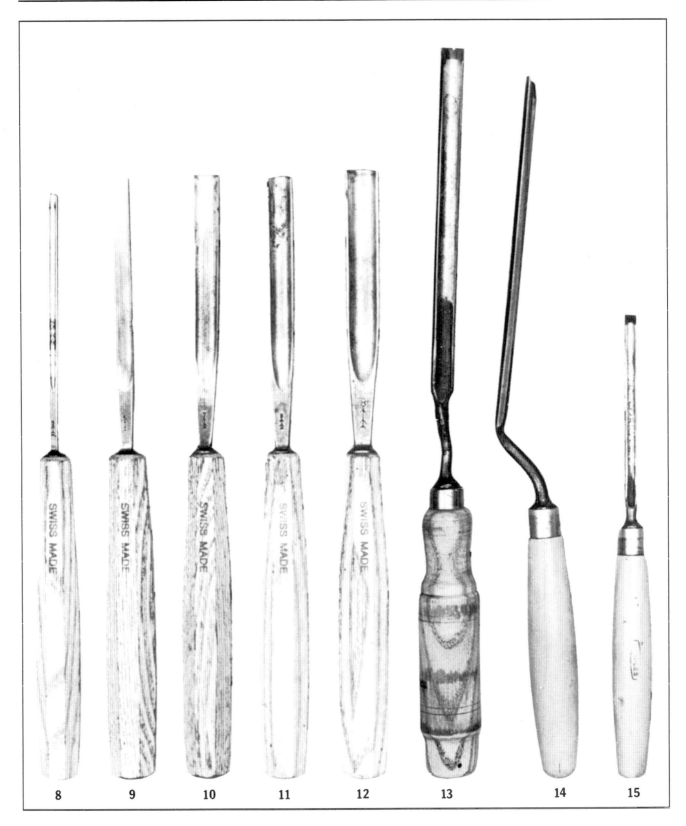

8) No. 9 sweep 3mm gouge, 9) No. 5 sweep 8mm gouge, 10) No. 7 sweep 10mm gouge, 11) No. 8 sweep 10mm gouge, 12) No. 8 sweep 13mm gouge, 13) 1/2-inch dogleg in-cannel gouge, 14) 5/8-inch (16mm) dogleg in-cannel gouge, 15) 1/4-inch in-cannel gouge

Appendix II

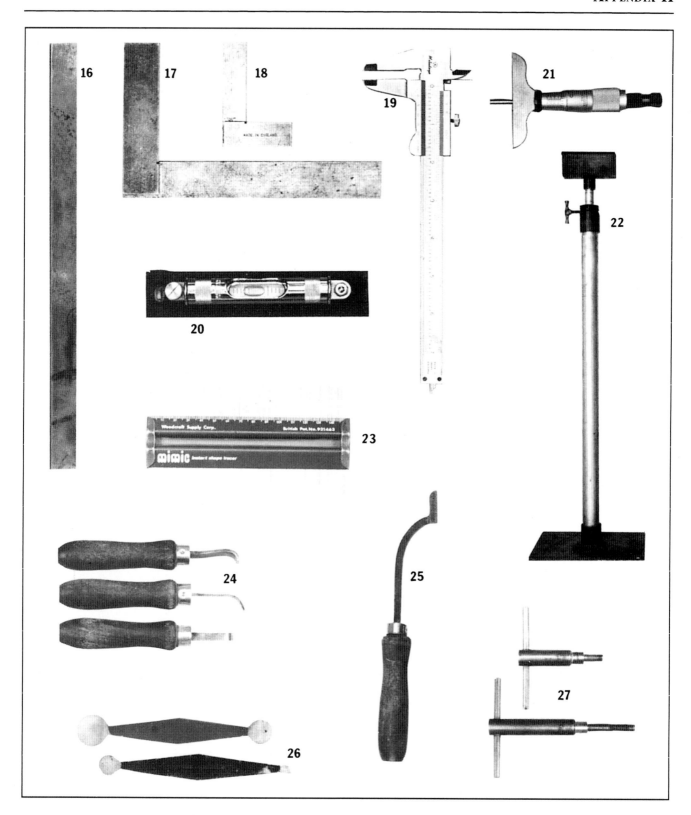

16) 1/8-inch x 18 inch ground die stock straightedge, 17) 6-inch precision square, 18) 2-1/2-inch precision square, 19) vernier calipers, 20) precision level, 21) depth micrometer, 22) "third-leg" support stand, 23) pattern maker template gauge, 24) flat scrapers (set of three), 25) Bull-foot bottoming file, 26) Fisher inletting scrapers, 27) stockmaker's hand screws (various actions),

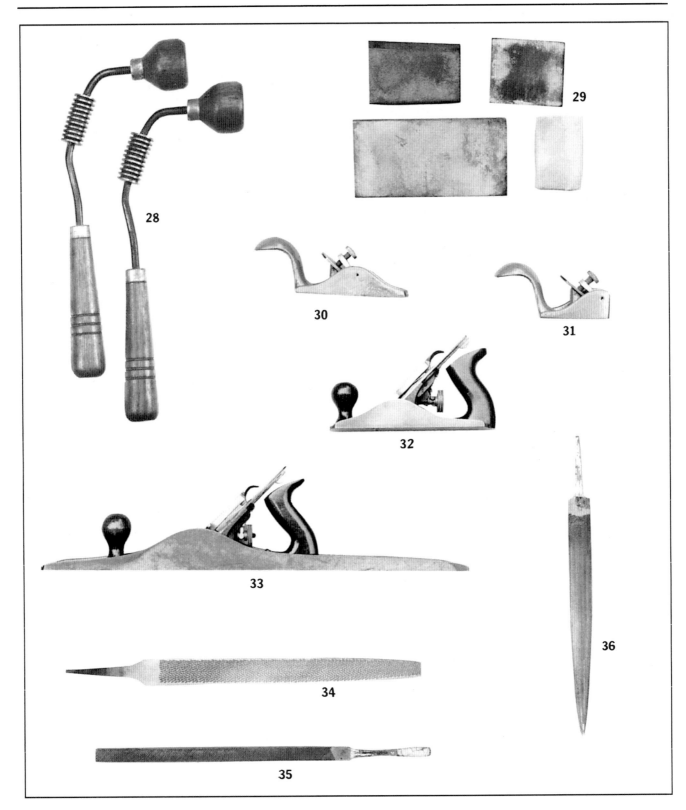

28) barrel-channel scrapers (1/2″, 9/16″, 5/8″, 11/16″, and 3/4″) available singly or in sets, 29) Shaped felt sanding blocks (set of 4), 30) 3-inch palm plane, 31) 2-inch Bull-nose plane, 32) 9-1/2-inch smooth plane, 33) 24-inch jointer plane, 34) Nicholson #50 patternmakers rasp, 35) Square file, 36) "O" cut crossing file.

APPENDIX II

A partial list of tool suppliers:

Brownells, Inc.
200 South Front Street
Montezuma, Iowa 50171
www.brownells.com
(chisels, scrapers)

Cooper Tools
P.O. Box 728 - 1000 Lufkin Road
Apex, North Carolina 27502
www.cooperhandtools.com
(files, rasps)

Constantine's
1040 East Oakland Park Boulevard
Ft. Lauderdale, Florida 33334
www.constantines.com
(chisels, planes, finishes)

Frank Mittermeier, Inc.
P.O. Box 2 - 3577 East Tremont Avenue
Bronx, New York 10465
www.dastrausa.com
(chisels, scrapers)

Woodworkers Supply
1108 North Glenn Road
Casper, Wyoming 82601
www.woodworker.com
(woodworking vises)

ACKNOWLEDGMENTS

The author would like to thank the following individuals for the encouragement and help that they have given him both in his career as a stockmaker/photographer and in the preparation of this book.

Mr. Jack T. Haugh, Dr. Ken Howell, Christene Keith, Mr. Frederick Sommer, Dr. Edward C. Ezell, James and Susan Weimer, Gary Kent, Col. Dick Kayser, Don and Norma Allen, Joseph B. Roberts Jr., John Bivins, Monte Mandarino, Mark Silver, Ed Webber, Richard Schreiber, Bruce Farnam, and Alex Butler.

A special acknowledgment and thank you goes to the following: Mr. Randy Swedlund — For opening up your darkroom to me those many years ago and for the excellent job you did in printing the black and white negatives for this book. Trinka M. Simon — For the many hours and late nights that you spent typing and trying to decipher the author's handwriting. For your cheerful attitude in putting up with the author's many changes and revisions of the material. For your comments and suggestions that helped take this project from a rough, handwritten manuscript to a finished text. Mr. Mark Harris — For having faith in my visions and for sending enough money to keep the author in beans and jeans for the last two years of this project.

This book would not have been possible without the help of the three of you. Thank you.